GAME DAY
NORTH CAROLINA
BASKETBALL

GAME DAY
NORTH CAROLINA
BASKETBALL

*The Greatest Games, Players, Coaches and Teams
in the Glorious Tradition of Tar Heel Basketball*

TRIUMPH
B O O K S
CHICAGO

Athlon Sports
AMERICA'S PREMIER SPORTS ANNUALS

Library of Congress Control Number: 2005908138

This book is available in quantity at special discounts for your group or organization.
For further information, contact:

Triumph Books
542 South Dearborn Street
Suite 750
Chicago, Illinois 60605
(312) 939-3330
Fax (312) 663-3557

EDITORS: Rob Doster, Mitchell Light

PHOTO EDITOR: Tim Clark

DESIGN: Anderson Thomas Design

PHOTO CREDITS: Bruce Schwartzman, NCAA Photos/Rich Clarkson, North Carolina Sports Information, Getty Images, AP Wide World

Printed in U.S.A.

ISBN-13: 978-1-57243-793-7
ISBN-10: 1-57243-793-6

CONTENTS

"When I arrived at school in the fall of 1990, it was immediately apparent that college basketball was king in the state of North Carolina, and with good reason." ERIC MONTROSS

Foreword

There is a Carolina blue line painted 10 inches wide at the players' entrance to the court at the Dean E. Smith Center. This line goes unnoticed by most, but to the Carolina men's basketball team, it marks the point at which competition begins, and focus becomes a necessity. I was told early on as a freshman at Carolina that this line was only to be crossed with both shoes tied, practice jersey tucked in, and mind prepared for practice. A light blue stripe of paint is not magical, but it created a mindset for all the players under the tutelage of coach Dean Smith. After all, the success of North Carolina did not come without focus and direction by the players and coaches. As new coaches like Bill Guthridge, Matt Doherty and Roy Williams have continued to contribute to the Carolina tradition, this line and the philosophy it represents have remained.

I grew up in Indiana, a hotbed of basketball. I was naïve to Carolina basketball and the scope of emotion and amount of pride associated with it. When I arrived at school in the fall of 1990, it was immediately apparent that college basketball was king in the state of North Carolina, and with good reason. The Tar Heel state hosted fierce ACC competition and was home to collegiate basketball's greatest rivalry: Carolina versus Duke.

Despite the state's justified obsession with the sport, Coach Smith established the legacy of Carolina coaches who have consistently taught and cared about more than just the game of basketball. The emphasis was on transforming young athletes into mature and educated adults of good character, both on and off the court. In my experience, this perspective was emphasized by the unique way that Coach Smith began each of our practices. Instead of beginning in a typical fashion with layup lines or fast-break drills, every Dean Smith practice started with a thought for the day, an impressive mix of life lessons and messages pertinent to the game of basketball. One such quote, which I have kept with me now for 15 years, reads: "When trying to move a mountain, you must first begin by removing small stones." Often the freshmen would be called upon to recite these lines, and if the player did not know the quote, the entire team would be sent to the end line to run sprints — that is, the entire team minus the player who made the mistake.

The personal transformation that takes place as a Carolina player is evident in the responsibility and respect given to the team's seniors. I remember arriving as a freshman in Chapel Hill to a team with King Rice, Pete Chilcutt and Rick Fox as the senior leaders. One of the days after preseason workouts, they were called into Ken Crowder's equipment room. That was a bit out of the ordinary, and so I asked what they were doing. They replied in a matter-of-fact response that they were picking out uniforms for the coming sea-

son. As if that were not enough, at times they were able to choose where the team ate, the hotels in which we stayed, and made many other day-to-day decisions. Coach Smith was, in a subtle way, empowering them to make good choices by relying on the teaching they had experienced in the previous three years to guide them.

In my mind, the success of men's basketball at the University of North Carolina is not a result of the talent of the players, but rather the ability of those players to make decisions — on and off the court — as a high-performing, cohesive unit. And because of the consistently excellent caliber of the coaching staff, these decisions draw from the lessons of college basketball's greatest mentors.

During my career in the NBA, teammates from other universities often asked me what it was that drew players back to UNC in the offseason. My explanation was simple: we are a family at Carolina. For students, four years spent in Chapel Hill create a bond, but for us, the bond was made stronger by every member of the basketball program, from assistant coaches to office personnel. Long after we have turned in our Carolina blue

jerseys, players are welcomed back to a place where there is a genuine interest in our lives after college.

As a senior in high school after committing to play basketball at the University of North Carolina, I bought a shirt that read on the back: "A tradition of excellence...the tradition continues." Below the quote was a picture of the Smith Center. A scholarship to play basketball at the University of North Carolina was a chance to be a part of this rich tradition. Basketball may bring us to Chapel Hill, but we leave with so much more. We leave with a broader outlook on life and effective ways to handle it, a formal education and a way to use it and a lifelong bond to the tradition of excellence.

—ERIC MONTROSS

Introduction

The images are unforgettable and too numerous to count. James Worthy throwing down thunderous dunks against the vaunted Georgetown defense. A freshman named Michael Jordan stroking a sweet jump shot that helps launch him into immortality. Phil Ford dissecting the defenses of the ACC with the precision of a surgeon. Frank McGuire's Tar Heels giving the nation a lesson in heart during a grueling NCAA Tournament run. Sean May and Co. restoring Carolina to its rightful place atop the college hoops world. The incomparable Dean Smith running his program with class and excellence. Roy Williams grabbing the mantle carrying it into a new century.

We're taking the history, drama and pageantry of North Carolina basketball and distilling them into the pages that follow. It's a daunting task. Few basketball programs in the country inspire the loyalty and passion that Carolina elicits from its fans, and with good reason.

Through the words and images we present, we hope you will get a taste of what Tar Heel basketball is all about. Decades have passed since players first donned the Carolina blue, but one thing hasn't changed: Tar Heel basketball is a tradition, a legacy of greatness, a way of life.

TRADITIONS AND PAGEANTRY

The sights and sounds of Game Day in Chapel Hill create an unmatched spectacle, a glorious mix of tradition and color and pomp and pageantry. Here's a small sample of what makes North Carolina basketball unique.

The Nickname

It's fitting that North Carolina's athletic teams are nicknamed the Tar Heels. After all, they hail from the Tar Heel state. But just where did that moniker come from?

One legend credits a Revolutionary War incident for giving birth to the nickname. As the troops of British General Cornwallis were fording what is now known as the Tar

River in the area between Rocky Mount and Battleboro, they found their way impeded by gooey tar that had been dumped in the water. Reputedly, those troops made the observation that anyone fording rivers in North Carolina would wind up with tar on their heels.

Others credit an incident in the Civil War. During a fierce fight, a column that was supporting North Carolina troops was routed and fled. After the battle, the North Carolinians who had been left behind but fought successfully met up with the fleeing regiment and were met with the question, "Any more tar down in the Old North State, boys?"

"No, not a bit. Old Jeff's bought it all up," a North Carolinian replied, referring to Confederate President Jefferson Davis.

"Is that so? What's he going to do with it?"

"He's going to put it on you'ns heels to make you stick better in the next fight."

When he heard about the incident, Robert E. Lee remarked, "God bless the Tar Heel boys."

There may be another, simpler explanation. An 1864 letter from Maj. Joseph Engelhard recounts a battle involving men from North Carolina in which Lee was heard to have said, "There they stand as if they have tar on their heels."

The Colors

When the University reopened after the Civil War, the Dialectic and Philanthropic literary societies directed most of the school's social activities. Membership in one or the other was mandatory for all students. The official color of the Di was light blue and that of the Phi white. It was the custom for all men from west of Chapel Hill to affiliate with the Di and for students from the east to become members of the Phi.

On public occasions the student officers, marshals and ball managers were chosen equally from the membership of the two societies. While students wore their society color on such occasions, the chief marshal and chief ball manager, one from the Di and the other from the Phi, wore both colors, signifying that they represented the whole student body.

With the advent of intercollegiate athletics, it seemed natural for the fans to wear the same combination of colors as that used by the chief marshals and ball managers, colors that represented not membership in a society, but a unified University student body. The athletic teams soon followed suit.

The Ram

A ram may seem like an odd mascot for athletic teams nicknamed the Tar Heels, but the strong, proud and stubborn animal has prowled the Carolina sidelines for more than eight decades.

Here's how Vic Huggins, Carolina's head cheerleader in 1924, explained the adoption of the ram mascot: "In 1924 school spirit was at a peak. But something seemed to be missing. One day it hit me. Georgia had a bulldog for a mascot and (North Carolina) State a wolf. What Carolina needed was a symbol."

Huggins found that symbol by looking to the football team's recent past. A star of the 1922 Tar Heel football squad that finished 9-1 was a rugged fullback named Jack Merritt, who was nicknamed "the battering ram" for the way he pounded opposing lines. And Huggins had his inspiration.

"Charlie Woollen, the athletic business manager at that time, agreed with the idea and gave us $25 to purchase a fitting mascot," said Huggins.

Rameses the First arrived from Texas in time for the game with a strong VMI squad. After a stirring pep rally, the ram made his way to Emerson Field, where Carolina was a decided underdog against the Keydets.

After three quarters, the game was still scoreless. Late in the fourth quarter, Carolina's Bunn Hackney was called upon to attempt a field goal. Before taking the field he stopped to rub Rameses' head for good luck.

Seconds later Hackney's 30-yard kick split the uprights, giving the Tar Heels a 3-0 victory, and a legendary mascot was born.

THE GREATEST PLAYERS

North Carolina basketball has seen its share of legends. The names are familiar to fans of college basketball, and for the fans of Carolina's rivals, they still bring a shiver of dread.

CARTWRIGHT CARMICHAEL
F/G, 1922-24

The first North Carolina athlete to become an All-American in any sport, Carmichael received those honors in 1923 and 1924. He and his brother, Billy, formed North Carolina's first basketball brother combination in 1922. North Carolina went 56-7 in Carmichael's three seasons, winning the national championship as voted by the Helms Foundation when North Carolina went undefeated (26–0) in 1923-24.

Carmichael displayed his sportsmanship in the Southern Conference championship game in 1924, according to the *Charlotte Observer*. With North Carolina ahead late in the game, Slim Carter fouled out, leaving Alabama with only four players to finish the game. Carmichael objected, Carter was allowed to return and North Carolina finished off a 26–18 victory.

JACK COBB
F, 1924-26

North Carolina's first National Player of the Year, Cobb received that honor from the Helms Foundation in 1926. He helped lead the Tar Heels to a 66–10 record over three seasons, including 26–0 in 1923-24, when the Helms foundation named North Carolina national champion. Cobb, whose nickname was "Mr. Basketball," was a 6-foot-2 forward who could pass, rebound and especially score. North Carolina's first three-time All-American, Cobb lost part of his left leg in an automobile crash shortly after graduating.

"Glamack night after night, with seldom an interlude of coolness, *bats the ball through the mesh suffi-* *ciently often to give the Phantoms* *(North Carolina) a victory."*
COLUMNIST JAKE WADE IN THE
CHARLOTTE OBSERVER, FEB. 12, 1941

GEORGE GLAMACK
C, 1938-41

With World War II raging, this Pennsylvanian known as "The Blind Bomber" became the top player in college basketball. Glamack's poor eyesight kept him from focusing on the rim, so he used the lines on the court to guide his shot.

He shot the hook well with both hands from either side of the lane and had a pair of remarkable scoring performances in 1941. He scored 45 against Clemson and 31 against Dartmouth in the NCAA Tournament, a score not matched in NCAA play until 1952. Glamack averaged 17.6 points per game as a junior and 20.6 points as a senior, and was selected National Player of the Year by the Helms Foundation in both seasons. In 1941, his leadership propelled the Tar Heels to a Southern Conference title and North Carolina's first NCAA Tournament appearance.

LENNIE ROSENBLUTH
F, 1954-57

The most prolific scorer in North Carolina history on a per game basis, Rosenbluth was selected National Player of the Year by the Helms Foundation in 1957, the year the Tar Heels defeated Wilt Chamberlain and Kansas in triple overtime in the NCAA championship game.

Rosenbluth was a 6-foot-5 native of the Bronx, one of five starters on the NCAA championship team brought to North Carolina by former St. John's coach Frank McGuire on what became known as the Underground Railroad. His single-season scoring average of 28.0 points per game in 1956-57 and his career scoring average of 26.9 both are school records that have stood the test of time.

His 3-point play in the lane against Wake Forest in the ACC Tournament semifinals kept the Tar Heels undefeated en route to a 32–0 record and vaulted them into the NCAA Tournament on the way to the national title. "I was a very streaky shooter," Rosenbluth said. "I might miss three, four, five in a row. But I would come back and hit the next six or seven in a row."

BILLY CUNNINGHAM
F/C, 1962-65

Nicknamed The Kangaroo Kid for his outstanding jumping ability, Cunningham was a ferocious rebounder and skillful scorer at 6-foot-6. He was a two-time All-American and led the ACC in rebounding three straight seasons — one of only four players to do so. His career scoring average of 24.8 points is second in school history to Lennie Rosenbluth's 26.9. He went on to a successful 11-year pro career, winning an NBA title in 1976 with the Philadelphia 76ers, and perhaps is best known for his NBA coaching career. Cunningham's .698 winning percentage was second only to Phil Jackson's through 2004-05 among NBA coaches. Cunningham coached Julius Erving, Bobby Jones and the 76ers to an NBA championship in 1983.

"He communicated well. He was very much a competitor. . . . He'd been retired 10 or 15 years and we were in Phoenix. . .and someone asked if he could still dunk the ball. I'd hardly ever seen him shoot the ball. And he went up and just threw it down pretty hard." BOBBY JONES

"Larry Miller was like the Pete Rose type. Larry was Mr. Hustle. He was a left-hander. He was a banger. He was not the most talented player. He was just a winner, a banger. Beautiful, left-handed stroke. He was one of Dean Smith's first prototype players." FORMER GEORGIA TECH COACH BOBBY CREMINS

BOB LEWIS, F/G, 1964-67

By all rights, Lewis should have been too small to play in the frontcourt at 6-foot-3. But he was an incredible leaper who used that ability to score over bigger players in the post.

Lewis teamed with Billy Cunningham for a dynamic post tandem as a sophomore, then averaged 27.4 points per game — the second-highest season mark in school history — as a junior. Lewis unselfishly moved to guard and sacrificed his scoring as a senior, when he helped the Tar Heels finish first in the ACC, win the ACC Tournament and reach the Final Four. His scoring average of 22.1 points per game ranks third in school history, and he set the school single-game scoring record with 49 points against Florida State on

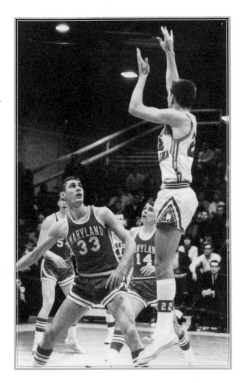

LARRY MILLER, G/F, 1965-68

North Carolina was struggling in the early 1960s in the opening years of Dean Smith's tenure until this strong-willed Pennsylvanian got the program back on track. Miller is North Carolina's only two-time ACC Player of the Year.

A left-handed shooter, he averaged more than 20 points per game in each of his three seasons. For his career, he averaged 21.8 points, and he scored 10 or more points in a school-record 64 consecutive games. Miller was incredibly effective on the boards considering that he was only 6-foot-4, averaging 9.2 rebounds per game.

Miller was a first-team All-American as a junior and senior. Most important, in both those seasons, the Tar Heels placed first in the ACC in the regular season and won the conference championship. They reached the Final Four in 1967 for the first time in 10 years and played in the NCAA title game in 1968.

CHARLIE SCOTT
G/F, 1967-70

The first black scholarship athlete in any sport at North Carolina, Scott was the perfect young man for his pioneering role. The New York City native was bright enough to be valedictorian at Laurinburg (N.C.) Institute and possessed an infectious smile and radiant personality that immediately made him likeable.

He also had the game to deflect any kind of criticism. Lanky and quick, Scott could score from anywhere on the court and still ranks fifth in school history with 2,007 career points. Scott helped North Carolina reach two Final Fours and was a first-team All-American in his senior season, when he averaged an ACC-high 27.1 points.

"When I would guard Charlie and he would take a jump shot, I would be looking at his belly button. He had a great off-the-dribble jumping ability. He could really get up. If he had a little room on that first dribble, he would just shoot right over me. He was a great athlete, great scorer and great driver." BOBBY CREMINS

"Playing at North Carolina, you recognize what your strengths and weaknesses are. I recognized that one of my strengths was playing defense. I could hit the open shot, but I really wasn't a guy that was going to get my own shot on a regular basis, so I just tried to concentrate on what I did well." BOBBY JONES

BOBBY JONES
F, 1971-74

Perhaps the best defensive player in North Carolina history, Jones used positioning, long arms and knowledge of the game to present a huge challenge for N.C. State's David Thompson, Maryland's Len Elmore and other players in the post. Jones also was ahead of his time on offense as a post player, handling the ball and passing well and shooting 60.8 percent from the field in his career.

As a senior, he stole an inbounds pass at Duke and drove the length of the floor for a layup at the buzzer to give North Carolina a 73–71 victory in one of the most memorable moments of the Tar Heels' storied series with the Blue Devils. He went on to make the NBA's all-defensive team in eight straight seasons and won an NBA championship with the Philadelphia 76ers in 1983 under another former Tar Heel, coach Billy Cunningham.

WALTER DAVIS, F, 1973-77

The skills of "Sweet D," as he was known to Tar Heel fans, were considerable. He was known mostly for his ability to score inside and out, as he went on to become the NBA's 17th-leading career scorer at the time of his retirement. But Davis also could play defense — he held N.C. State's David Thompson to 7-for-21 from the field in the ACC final in 1975. Davis' most famous shot came when he was a freshman, as he banked in a 35-footer to cap a rally from eight points down in 17 seconds against Duke as the Tar Heels went on to win in overtime. Davis won the NBA Rookie of the Year award in 1978 and was an All-Star five times in his 15-year NBA career.

"Walter was just a very smooth player. He had a very smooth stroke.

He had good quickness, didn't force a lot of shots, and had good strength to not lose his angle to the basket."

BOBBY JONES

PHIL FORD, G, 1974-78

It took a special player to become the first to start his first collegiate game for Dean Smith at North Carolina. Ford ran Smith's famous "Four Corners" stalling offense to near-perfection, driving defenders crazy with clever ball-handling in the middle of the floor while his teammates stood at the corners of the court, waiting for outlet passes. Ford scored 78 points in three games to win the 1975 ACC Tournament Most Valuable Player award and became North Carolina's leading career scorer with 2,290 points. He was a three-time first-team All-American, went on to become the NBA Rookie of the Year in 1979, and served as an assistant coach at North Carolina from 1988 to 2000.

AL WOOD, G/F, 1977-81

His career shooting percentage of .560 might be the most impressive thing about Wood's time at North Carolina. Keep in mind — Wood was not a post player and wasn't particularly athletic, so it wasn't as though he was dropping in all his baskets in the lane.

Instead, Wood had a fantastic jump shot that caused opponents fits. His 2,015 career points make him one of just five North Carolina players to exceed 2,000. As a senior, he led the Tar Heels to the 1981 NCAA title game against Indiana.

His most famous performance came in the Final Four against Virginia, when he scored 39 points to set a national semifinal record that still stands.

"That's about as fine an individual performance as I've ever seen in that particular game. He was just a great competitor and a great scorer." FORMER VIRGINIA COACH TERRY HOLLAND, ON AL WOOD'S 39-POINT OUTBURST IN THE 1981 NATIONAL SEMIFINALS

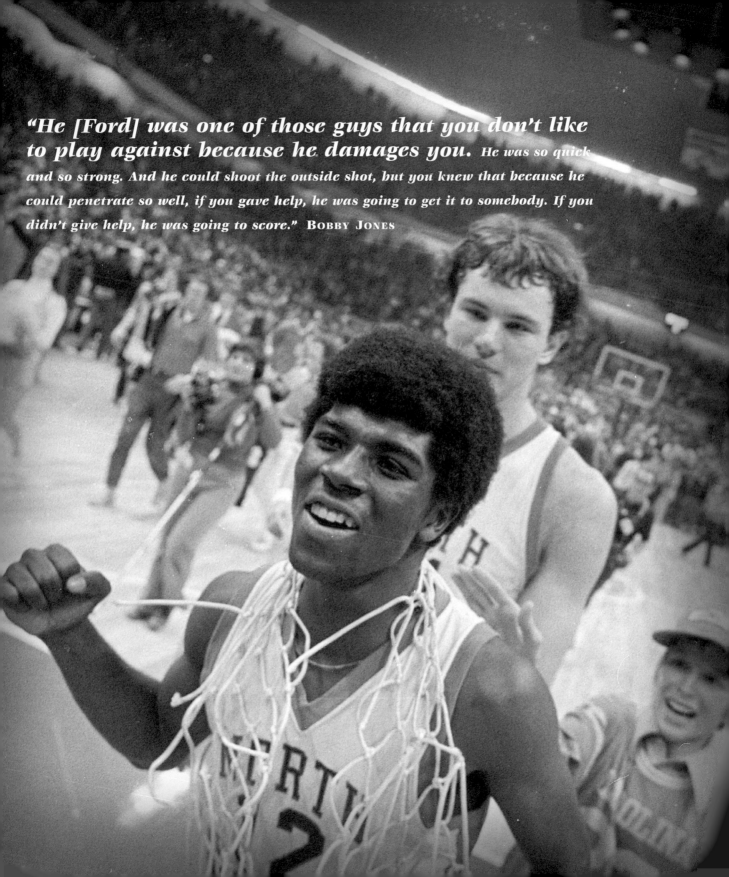

"He [Ford] was one of those guys that you don't like to play against because he damages you. *He was so quick and so strong. And he could shoot the outside shot, but you knew that because he could penetrate so well, if you gave help, he was going to get it to somebody. If you didn't give help, he was going to score."* BOBBY JONES

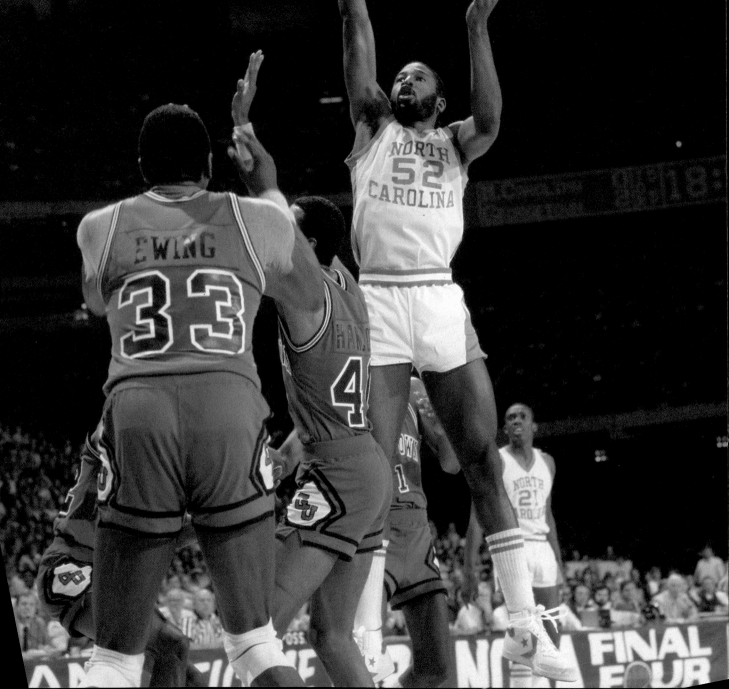

JAMES WORTHY, F, 1979-82

One of the most memorable moments in college basketball history was Worthy's interception of Fred Brown's ill-conceived pass in the closing seconds of North Carolina's 63–62 victory over Georgetown in the 1982 NCAA title game. It was fitting that the ball ended up in Worthy's hands, because he was named the MVP of the ACC Tournament that season and the Most Outstanding Player of the NCAA East Regional and the Final Four.

Worthy possessed a rare combination of strength, speed and quickness. He muscled inside for a .541 career field goal percentage as a Tar Heel, and after leaving North Carolina following his junior season, he ran the floor to finish with flourish on the receiving end of Magic Johnson's passes, as he won three NBA titles with the Los Angeles Lakers. Worthy became a seven-time NBA all-star.

★★★★★★★★★★★★★★★★★★★★★★★★★★★★★★★

SAM PERKINS, F/C, 1980-84

Known later in his pro career as "sleepy" Sam Perkins because of his heavy-lidded countenance, he played taller than his height at 6-foot-9 because of his long arms. It was said Perkins' sleeve length matched his jersey number — 41 — and he played some memorable games against Virginia's 7-foot-4 Ralph Sampson, helping hold him to 11 points in the national semifinals in 1981.

Perkins held the North Carolina career record with 245 blocked shots until Brendan Haywood passed him in 2001. He won an NCAA title in 1982 and is one of only four Tar Heels to be named a first-team All-American three times. He went on to a 17-year pro career, playing with the Los Angeles Lakers (1991), Seattle (1996) and Indiana (2000) in NBA championship series but never winning a title.

MICHAEL JORDAN
G, 1981-84

Regarded by most as the greatest player in basketball history and by some as the greatest athlete of the 20th century, Jordan was profoundly affected by his career at North Carolina and continues to regard the Tar Heel program with reverence. Though his fame necessarily has made him reclusive, he attended North Carolina's 75–70 victory over Illinois in the 2005 NCAA title game and celebrated with the players, coaches and Dean Smith in the locker room following the game. He has spoken often of how training under Smith helped him become a better player.

Though Jordan made the game-winning shot in the 1982 NCAA title game as a freshman and was National Player of the Year as a junior, his three-year college career wasn't quite as prolific as his pro career. He went on to win six NBA championships with the Chicago Bulls and won an NBA-record 10 scoring titles.

"Even though he was the unanimous National Player of the Year in 1984, no one could have imagined at the time he was in Chapel Hill the impact he would have on basketball, on sports in general and, really, the entire world. Yet he handled the attention as well as anyone could and genuinely remains surprised at all the attention he receives. I think that is a great trait among many he possesses." DEAN SMITH

BRAD DAUGHERTY
C, 1982-86

A prolific scorer in the post, Daugherty succeeded with a feathery shooting touch and excellent footwork. But he was just 16 when he arrived at North Carolina, and it took time for him to develop his screen-setting and rebounding skills.

By the time he was a junior, he had developed the physical strength to complement his well-developed scoring skills. Daugherty had excellent hands and rarely dropped a pass when his teammates fed him in the post. He shot 62 percent from the field for his career, and was a first-team All-American as a senior.

Daugherty was drafted No. 1 in 1986 by the Cleveland Cavaliers and became a five-time All-Star. The Tar Heels were 111–26 during his four seasons on the team.

"He's called 'The Jet' for a reason. I used to do preseason conditioning. We'd do 220-yard sprints. Kenny did it so well, quickly, fast, that the track coach at North Carolina got him to run in a couple of track meets. The other team could score and we'd get it out of bounds quickly and get it to Kenny. He used such speed, sometimes even after a made basket, he could lay it up on the other end."* ROY WILLIAMS

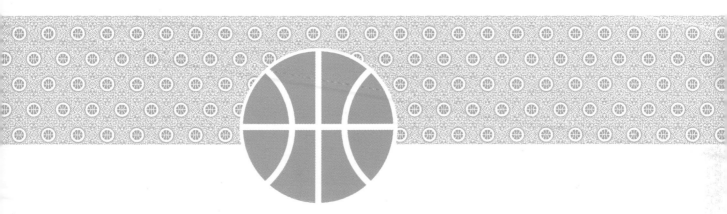

KENNY SMITH
G, 1983-87

Whereas Phil Ford became well known for running the Four Corners stall as a point guard, Smith made his mark with his incredible speed. With Smith leading the fast break as a senior in 1986-87, the Tar Heels set a school record that still stands by averaging 91.3 points per game. Smith ranks second in North Carolina history with 768 assists and fourth with 195 steals, and his pull-up jump shooting ability prevented opponents from sagging into the lane to stop him from distributing the ball. He was a first-team All-American as a senior, when *Basketball Times* named him National Player of the Year.

*"**I have to take it as a compliment.** I think everybody knows Michael Jordan is the greatest player. For people to think that we have some things in common, gives me a lot of encouragement, and a lot of confidence. But I still think that I have my own style of playing and I think we do do some things similar, but basically it's almost a totally different game." JERRY STACKHOUSE AT THE 1995 FINAL FOUR*

JERRY STACKHOUSE
F, 1993-95

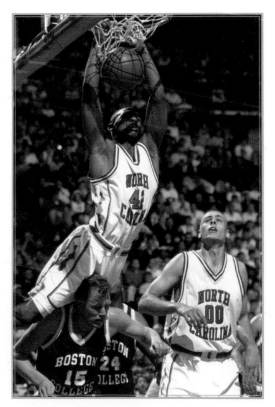

One of the most highly regarded wing players ever to come out of the state of North Carolina, the Kinston native became one of four freshmen to win ACC Tournament Most Valuable Player honors. As a sophomore, Stackhouse was a first-team All-American and was named National Player of the Year by *Sports Illustrated.* His ability to score from the perimeter, on mid-range pull-up jumpers and drives to the basket made him a complete player on offense. He also hit the boards hard, averaging 8.2 rebounds as a sophomore before leaving North Carolina for the NBA after just two seasons. He made his former North Carolina coaches proud when he received his degree in African Studies in December of 1999 despite having spent just two seasons at the school.

He was sometimes compared to Michael Jordan but humble enough to know he wasn't nearly the equal of the game's greatest player.

SEAN MAY, C, 2002-05

This Bloomington, Ind., native broke the hearts of Indiana fans by choosing North Carolina instead of the Hoosiers, whom his father, Scott, led to the NCAA title as the National Player of the Year in 1976. In his third and final season, Sean May added another NCAA championship to the family cache as he was named Most Outstanding Player of the Final Four. After a substandard sophomore season, May devoted himself to changing his body through a rigorous offseason running and lifting regimen. He averaged a team-high 17.5 points and 10.7 rebounds in his junior season.

"I've had guys work on their shot before, and they are working on the dribbling or something like that. But he just spent so much time trying to be a better athlete and a more conditioned athlete. And I think that his success is directly related to that hard work that he put in." ROY WILLIAMS

ANTAWN JAMISON, F, 1995-98

Though teammate Vince Carter often made more spectacular plays than Jamison during their concurrent, three-year careers, Jamison was more productive. The Charlotte native parked his 6-foot-9 frame on the block and scored with an exquisite variety of post moves, helping the Tar Heels reach two Final Fours. In his junior season, Jamison was named National Player of the Year after averaging 22.2 points and 10.5 rebounds per game. His scoring average was North Carolina's highest in 28 years, and he set the school record for rebounds in a season with 389, breaking Billy Cunningham's record of 379 set in 1964.

Other Carolina Greats

JOHN DILLON
F, 1944-48

Nicknamed "Hook," Dillon was an All-American in 1946 and 1947 and was the leading scorer on the 1946 team, North Carolina's first to reach the Final Four.

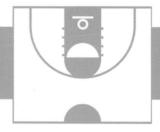

PETE BRENNAN
F, 1955-58

A member of the 1957 NCAA championship team, he averaged 21.3 points and was a first-team All-American the following season.

LEE SHAFFER
F, 1957-60

Shaffer was the ACC Player of the Year and a first-team All-American in 1959-60.

BOB MCADOO

F/C, 1971-72

In his one season with the Tar Heels, McAdoo averaged 19.5 points and led the team to the Final Four. He became the first North Carolina player to enter the draft with college eligibility remaining.

DOUG MOE

A first-team All-American in 1960-61, Moe coached 15 seasons in the NBA and was named the NBA Coach of the Year with the Denver Nuggets in 1988.

MITCH KUPCHAK
F, 1955-58

The first freshman to play basketball at North Carolina after the freshman eligibility rule went into effect, he earned ACC Player of the Year honors in 1975-76.

J.R. REID
F/C, 1986-89

Solidly built and deceptively quick, Reid was a two-time All-American.

MIKE O'KOREN

F, 1976-80

A three-time first-team All-American, he was a rare four-year starter for the Tar Heels.

JOSEPH FORTE

G, 1999-2001

Averaged 20.9 points and was a first-team All-American and co-ACC Player of the Year as a sophomore with Duke's Shane Battier.

THE GREATEST COACHES

North Carolina basketball has been blessed with some of the game's greatest tacticians, motivators and leaders. Three names rise to the top of the list, led by the game's all-time winningest coach.

Dean Smith
1961-97

Taking over for a legend is never easy. Just ask Dean Smith. Long before he built his own legacy in Chapel Hill, Smith had the difficult task of replacing the highly successful Frank McGuire, who led the Tar Heels to five ACC titles and the 1957 national championship in his nine years at North Carolina.

DEAN SMITH YEAR BY YEAR

YEAR	OVERALL W-L	PCT.	ACC W-L	ACC FINISH	ACC TOURN.	POSTSEASON MEDIA	RANK COACHES	POSTSEASON FINISH
1961-62	8-9	.471	7-7	Tied 4th	Quarterfinalist			
1962-63	15-6	.714	10-4	3rd	Semifinalist			
1963-64	12-12	500	6-8	5th	Semifinalist			
1964-65	15-9	.625	10-4	Tied 2nd	Quarterfinalist			
1965-66	16-11	.593	8-6	Tied 3rd	Semifinalist			
1966-67	26-6	.813	12-2	1st	Champion	4th	3rd	NCAA 4th
1967-68	28-4	.875	12-2	1st	Champion	4th	4th	NCAA Finalist
1968-69	27-5	.844	12-2	1st	Champion	4th	2nd	NCAA 4th
1969-70	18-9	.667	9-5	Tied 2nd	Quarterfinalist			NIT Final 16
1970-71	26-6	.813	11-3	1st	Finalist	13th	13th	NIT Champion
1971-72	26-5	.839	9-3	1st	Champion	2nd	2nd	NCAA 3rd
1972-73	25-8	.758	8-4	2nd	Quarterfinalist	11th	12th	NIT 3rd
1973-74	22-6	.786	9-3	Tied 2nd	Semifinalist	12th	8th	NIT Final 16
1974-75	23-8	.742	8-4	Tied 2nd	Champion	9th	10th	NCAA Final 16
1975-76	25-4	.862	11-1	1st	Finalist	8th	6th	NCAA Final 32
1976-77	28-5	.848	9-3	1st	Champion	5th	3rd	NCAA Finalist
1977-78	23-8	.742	9-3	1st	Semifinalist	16th	10th	NCAA Final 32
1978-79	23-6	.793	9-3	Tied 1st	Champion	9th	3rd	NCAA Final 32
1979-80	21-8	.724	9-5	Tied 2nd	Semifinalist	15th	15th	NCAA Final 32
1980-81	29-8	.784	10-4	2nd	Champion	6th	6th	NCAA Finalist
1981-82	32-2	.941	12-2	Tied 1st	Champion	1st	1st	NCAA Champion
1982-83	28-8	.778	12-2	Tied 1st	Semifinalist	8th	8th	NCAA Final 8
1983-84	28-3	.903	14-0	1st	Semifinalist	1st	1st	NCAA Final 16
1984-85	27-9	.750	9-5	Tied 1st	Finalist	7th	7th	NCAA Final 8
1985-86	28-6	.824	10-4	3rd	Quarterfinalist	8th	8th	NCAA Final 16
1986-87	32-4	.889	14-0	1st	Finalist	2nd	3rd	NCAA Final 8
1987-88	27-7	.794	11-3	1st	Finalist	7th	8th	NCAA Final 8
1988-89	29-8	.784	9-5	2nd	Champion	5th	4th	NCAA Final 16
1989-90	21-13	.618	8-6	Tied 3rd	Quarterfinalist			NCAA Final 16
1990-91	29-6	.829	10-4	2nd	Champion	4th	4th	NCAA Final 4
1991-92	23-10	.697	9-7	3rd	Finalist	18th	12th	NCAA Final 16
1992-93	34-4	.895	14-2	1st	Finalist	4th	1st	NCAA Champion
1993-94	28-7	.800	11-5	2nd	Champion	1st	9th	NCAA Final 32
1994-95	28-6	.823	12-4	Tied 1st	Finalist	4th	3rd	NCAA Final 4
1995-96	21-11	.656	10-6	3rd	Quarterfinalist	25th	24th	NCAA Final 32
1996-97	28-7	.800	11-5	Tied 2nd	Champion	4th	4th	NCAA Semifinalist
Totals	879-254	.776	364-136					

Smith's early years as a head coach were a struggle; his first team went 8–9; his third team 12–12; and during his fourth season, in 1965, Smith was hung in effigy on the UNC campus during a midseason losing streak.

Well, it's a good thing the North Carolina administration showed some patience with its young head coach. Smith quickly righted the ship, and in the late 1960s, Carolina re-emerged as the dominant program in the highly regarded ACC with three straight league titles and three straight trips to the Final Four. From that point, Carolina made a habit of winning at the highest level. From 1966 through his retirement in 1997, Smith averaged 26.2 wins per season and won fewer than 20 games just once — an 18-win season in 1969-70. Under his watch, the Tar

I knew when I signed with North Carolina that I was getting a great coach for four years, but, in addition, I got a great friend for a lifetime." PHIL FORD

Heels won 17 regular-season ACC titles, 13 ACC Tournament titles and appeared in the NCAA Tournament 27 times. The big prize,  the national title, eluded Smith for the first two decades of his career, but the Tar Heels broke through in 1982 with a memorable win over Georgetown and won another crown in 1993 by defeating Michigan.

Smith retired in 1997 with 879 wins, the most by any Division I head coach in the history of the sport.

"What's more impressive to me about Dean than his record is how good he is as a teacher of basketball," said fellow Hall of Famer John Wooden. "I've always said that he's a better teacher of basketball than anyone else."

A MODEL OF CONSISTENCY

A small sample of Dean Smith's unmatched record of consistent excellence:

- Smith's Tar Heel teams won at least 20 games for 27 straight years and 30 of his final 31. No other coach has even won 20 games for 27 years.
- Smith boasted an NCAA-record 22 seasons with at least 25 wins.
- From 1981 to 1989, Carolina was ranked in the final top 10 of both the Associated Press and coaches' polls each year.
- The Tar Heels were ranked among the nation's final top 15 teams 28 of Smith's last 31 seasons, missing only in 1970, 1990 and 1996. Smith teams finished the season ranked No. 1 in at least one of the two major polls four times (1982, 1984, 1993 and 1994).
- Under Smith, the Heels had a record of 364-136 in ACC regular-season play, a winning percentage of .728.
- The Tar Heels finished no worse than third in the ACC regular-season standings for 33 successive seasons under Smith. In that span, Carolina finished first 17 times, second 11 times and third five times.

Frank McGuire
1952-61

North Carolina basketball was at a crossroads following the 1951-52 season. The once-dominant Tar Heels had struggled through their second consecutive 12–15 season and stumbled to 11th place in the Southern Conference standings.

Tom Scott was out after just six seasons as UNC's head coach. The next hire was crucial, and the Carolina administration delivered 38-year-old Frank McGuire from St. John's University. A New York City native, McGuire averaged 25 wins in his final three seasons

with the Redmen. His next challenge was to restore order in Chapel Hill and return the Tar Heels to national prominence.

He did just that, though it took a few years longer than most Carolina faithful had hoped. McGuire's first team, the 1952-53 Tar Heels captained by Vincent Grimaldi and Jack Wallace, won 17 games and lost just 10. The next two years, however, produced mediocre records of 11–10 and 10–11 — not exactly what Carolina had in mind when McGuire was hired.

FRANK McGUIRE AT NORTH CAROLINA

YEAR	OVERALL RECORD		CONFERENCE		
1952-53	17–10	.630	15–6 (Southern)	8th	
1953-54	11–10	.523	5–6 (ACC)	5th	
1954-55	10–11	.476	8–6	T-4th	
1955-56	18–5	.783	11–3	1st	
1956-57	32–0	1.000	14–0	1st	National Champion
1957-58	19–7	.731	10–4	T-2nd	
1958–59	20–5	.800	12–2	1st	
1959-60	18–6	.750	12–2	1st	
1960–61	19–4	.826	12–2	1st	

Any questions regarding McGuire's ability to lead North Carolina to the top of the college basketball world ended shortly thereafter. The 1955-56 Tar Heels won 18 games and went 11–3 in conference play to capture the ACC regular-season title in the league's third year of existence. And that was just an appetizer. The next season, Carolina achieved something that every team dreams about but precious few attain — perfection. Led by All-America forward Lennie Rosenbluth, the Tar Heels went 24–0 in the regular season, 3–0 in the ACC Tournament and then won five straight in the NCAA Tournament to win the national title.

During his final four seasons in Chapel Hill, McGuire failed to lead Carolina back to the Final Four, but the Tar Heels continued to win big. They averaged 19 wins over that span and won the ACC regular-season title in 1959, '60 and '61. His final record in nine seasons at UNC was a sparkling 164–58, good for a .739 winning percentage.

McGuire's success in Chapel Hill can largely be attributed to his ability to convince players from his native New York to head south to play their college basketball. In fact, the entire starting five on Carolina's 1957 national title team called New York City home.

McGuire's greatest recruit, however, never played one game for the Tar Heels. Prior to the 1958-59 season, he hired a young assistant named Dean Smith, who went on to become arguably the greatest coach in the history of the game.

Roy Williams
2003-present

It took Roy Williams less than two years to cement his legacy as an all-time great at North Carolina. His name will forever be mentioned in the same breath as Frank McGuire and Dean Smith, two of the most successful coaches in the history of the sport.

Williams, a 1972 Carolina graduate, learned his craft while serving as Smith's assistant from 1978-88. He was an integral part of two Final Four teams, including the 1981-82 club that delivered the school's first national title in 25 years.

Williams went out on his own in 1988, taking over the storied Kansas Jayhawks after Larry Brown departed for the NBA's San Antonio Spurs. Williams enjoyed tremendous success at KU — he went 418–101 (.805) in 15 years — but the ultimate prize, a national championship, eluded him. He came painfully close, losing in the national title game in both 1991 and 2003, but never was able to cut down the nets on the game's greatest stage.

North Carolina attempted to lure Williams back home following Bill Guthridge's retire-

ment in 2000, but he made the difficult decision to remain at Kansas. The Tar Heels came calling once again after the 2002-03 season, and that time Williams was unable to say no to his beloved alma mater. Just two weeks after leading Kansas to the national title game, Williams was introduced as the next head coach of the North Carolina basketball program.

"I want to tell everyone in here there will never be a day when you think someone is working harder than your head basketball coach," Williams said at his introductory press conference. "And the players, there will never be a day when you think a head coach is working harder."

Williams inherited a Carolina program that was in the midst of a two-year NCAA Tournament drought, the school's longest since the early 1970s.

His first team won 19 games but was a rather ordinary 8–8 in the ACC and bowed out of the NCAA Tournament in the second round. There was, however, nothing ordinary about the next season. Loaded with a roster considered by many to be the most talented in the nation, the Tar Heels rolled through the ACC with a 14–2 record and received a No. 1 seed in the NCAA Tournament. Six wins later, Williams' dream finally became a reality — a national championship as the head coach at North Carolina.

"He is the greatest coach," said Raymond Felton, the Tar Heels' starting point guard. "If he retired tomorrow, I would vote for him for the Hall of Fame. He told us he would bring us a championship, and we did it as a team."

ROY WILLIAMS AT NORTH CAROLINA

YEAR	OVERALL RECORD		CONFERENCE	
2003-04	19–11	.633	8–8	5th
2004-05	33–4	.892	14–2	1st

THE CHAMPIONSHIPS

NATIONAL CHAMPIONS 2004-05

As a jubilant Roy Williams hugged a sweaty Sean May on the night of April 4, 2005 in St. Louis, a rebirth was completed.

Williams left Kansas to restore his alma mater to the glory it achieved for 36 years under Dean Smith. In Williams' second season, May's broad shoulders carried North Carolina on an NCAA title run that culminated in a 75–70 victory over Illinois in the championship game. It capped a remarkable turnaround for seniors Jawad Williams, Jackie Manuel and Melvin Scott, who as freshmen suffered one of the worst seasons in school history. North Carolina was 8–20 in 2001-02, and Williams was summoned to rescue the program after the Tar Heels went 19–16 in 2002-03, Matt Doherty's third season.

Doherty had recruited superior players who admittedly had difficulty putting aside their personal agendas for the good of the team. Roy Williams' first season at North Carolina was perhaps the most challenging of his coaching career, and though the Tar Heels reached the NCAA Tournament, they were bounced in the second round by Texas.

By the second season in Williams' system, the players had adjusted and began living up to their potential. After a shocking, season-opening loss to Santa Clara, North

Carolina captured the championship of the Maui Invitational and won 14 in a row.

Junior point guard Raymond Felton, perhaps the fastest player in college basketball, began making better decisions and thrived in Williams' up-tempo system. Wing Rashad McCants, known as much in the past for sulking and selfishness as for his sweet jump shot, played better defense and stopped forcing shots from the perimeter.

Freshman Marvin Williams, the overwhelming choice for ACC Rookie of the Year,

2004-05 RECORD: 34-4. ACC: 14-2

DATE	TEAM	WIN/LOSE	FINAL
Nov. 19	Santa Clara-a	L	77-66
Nov. 22	Brigham Young-b	W	86-50
Nov. 23	Tennessee-b	W	94-81
Nov. 24	Iowa-b	W	106-92
Nov. 28	Southern California	W	97-65
Dec. 1	at Indiana	W	70-63
Dec. 4	Kentucky	W	91-78
Dec. 12	Loyola-Chicago	W	109-60
Dec. 19	at Virginia Tech	W	85-51
Dec. 21	Vermont	W	93-65
Dec. 28	UNC Wilmington	W	96-75
Dec. 30	Cleveland State	W	107-64
Jan. 2	William & Mary	W	105-66
Jan. 8	Maryland	W	109-75
Jan. 12	Georgia Tech	W	91-69
Jan. 15	at Wake Forest	L	95-82
Jan. 19	at Clemson	W	77-58
Jan. 22	Miami	W	87-67
Jan. 29	at Virginia	W	110-76
Feb. 3	N.C. State	W	95-71
Feb. 6	at Florida State	W	81-60
Feb. 9	at Duke	L	71-70
Feb. 13	Connecticut-c	W	77-70
Feb. 16	Virginia	W	85-61
Feb. 19	Clemson	W	88-56
Feb. 22	at N.C. State	W	81-71
Feb. 27	at Maryland	W	85-83
March 3	Florida State	W	91-76
March 6	Duke	W	75-73

ACC TOURNAMENT

DATE	TEAM	WIN/LOSE	FINAL
March 11	Clemson-d	W	88-81
March 12	Georgia Tech-d	L	78-75

NCAA REGIONALS

DATE	TEAM	WIN/LOSE	FINAL
March 18	Oakland-e	W	96-68
March 20	Iowa State-e	W	92-65
March 25	Villanova-f	W	67-66
March 27	Wisconsin-f	W	88-82

NCAA FINAL FOUR

DATE	TEAM	WIN/LOSE	FINAL
April 2	Michigan State-g	W	87-71
April 4	Illinois-g	W	75-70

a-Oakland, Calif. b-Maui, Hawaii c- Hartford d- Washington, D.C
e- Charlotte f- Syracuse g- St. Louis

at once provided incredible depth and humility, coming off the bench to shine although he would prove to be the first player on the team chosen, No. 2 overall, in the NBA Draft.

May, the junior center, became the stabilizing force after reshaping his body with workmanlike focus on running and lifting weights during the offseason. May kept pace with the fast break and displayed newfound aggressiveness that, along with his soft hands, made him unstoppable on the boards.

In the regular-season finale, North Carolina erased a nine-point deficit in the final three minutes against Duke, scoring the final 11 points to win 75–73 as a Marvin Williams three-point play provided the go-ahead points as the Dean Smith Center erupted. The Tar Heels cut down the nets at the Smith Center after the victory over their rival gave them first place outright in the ACC standings.

North Carolina was eliminated in the ACC Tournament semifinals by Georgia Tech, but the best was yet to come. The Tar Heels breezed past Oakland and Iowa State in their first two NCAA Tournament games, before things got a little tougher. The Heels stopped Villanova after a controversial trav-

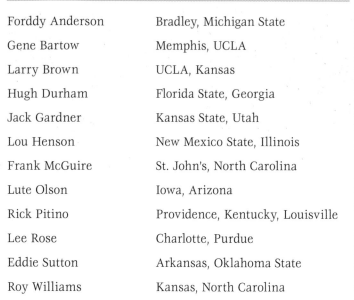

ROY WILLIAMS is one of 12 coaches to take at least two different teams to the Final Four (and the second from North Carolina):

COACH	SCHOOLS
Forddy Anderson	Bradley, Michigan State
Gene Bartow	Memphis, UCLA
Larry Brown	UCLA, Kansas
Hugh Durham	Florida State, Georgia
Jack Gardner	Kansas State, Utah
Lou Henson	New Mexico State, Illinois
Frank McGuire	St. John's, North Carolina
Lute Olson	Iowa, Arizona
Rick Pitino	Providence, Kentucky, Louisville
Lee Rose	Charlotte, Purdue
Eddie Sutton	Arkansas, Oklahoma State
Roy Williams	Kansas, North Carolina

eling call, and beat Wisconsin to reach the Final Four despite Felton's foul trouble.

A stellar second half eliminated Michigan State in the semifinals, leaving North Carolina in a highly anticipated meeting with Illinois, which had lost once in 38 games. Williams made a go-ahead tip-in with 1:26

remaining, and Felton stole a pass and made three free throws to seal the victory.

In the locker room, former Tar Heel luminaries Dean Smith and Michael Jordan celebrated with the players. The program they loved was on solid footing again, and they had the hardware to prove it.

NATIONAL CHAMPIONS 1992-93

Though the 1993 NCAA championship game is best remembered for Chris Webber's gaffe, there is little question that the North Carolina team that took advantage was a worthy champion.

With Michigan trailing 73–71 in the final 20 seconds, Webber dribbled into a corner, got trapped, and signaled timeout in an effort to get himself out of a jam. Problem was, the Wolverines had used all their timeouts. The resulting technical foul immediately ended Michigan's last-gasp comeback attempt, and the Tar Heels won 77–71, capturing coach Dean Smith's second NCAA title.

It was a much different team from Smith's previous champion from 1982, which boasted future NBA greats Michael Jordan, James Worthy and Sam Perkins. The 1993 Tar Heels were a more workmanlike bunch who won because they never strayed from their roles.

DEAN SMITH won his second NCAA title as a coach in 1992-93. He is one of 11 coaches with two or more titles:

COACH	SCHOOL	NCAA TITLES
John Wooden	UCLA	10
Adolph Rupp	Kentucky	4
Bob Knight	Indiana	3
Mike Krzyzewski	Duke	3
Jim Calhoun	Connecticut	2
Denny Crum	Louisville	2
Henry Iba	Oklahoma State	2
Ed Jucker	Cincinnati	2
Branch McCracken	Indiana	2
Dean Smith	North Carolina	2
Phil Woolpert	San Francicsco	2

Seven-foot Eric Montross was a throwback at center, staying on the block and using his height and muscle to wear down opponents. Derrick Phelps was a pass-first point guard who played excellent defense and didn't mind leaving the scoring to others.

Wing Donald Williams was a shooter extraordinaire; the Final Four's most out-standing player scored 25 points in both the semifinals and the final. George Lynch was a grinder on the offensive boards at one forward, and Brian Reese used his considerable athletic ability to get to the basket from the other forward position.

The Tar Heels returned every key player except talented scoring guard Hubert Davis

from the previous season, when they lost 80–73 to Ohio State in the NCAA Tournament regional semifinals. North Carolina started fast on its way to a 34–4 record, with the only loss in its first 18 games coming when Michigan's Jalen Rose scored a last-second basket for a 79–78 decision at the Rainbow Classic in Hawaii.

Each of North Carolina's first five ACC opponents fell by at least 10 points before the Tar Heels staged one of the greatest comebacks in ACC history against Florida State on Jan. 27. Florida State led by 21 in the second half and by 19 with under nine minutes remaining, but North Carolina scored 24 of the last 28 points to win 82–77.

North Carolina won the ACC regular season title with a 14–2 conference record but slipped in the ACC Tournament final

1992-93 RECORD: 34-4. ACC: 14-2

DATE	TEAM	WIN/LOSE	FINAL
Dec. 1	Old Dominion	W	119-82
Dec. 4	South Carolina-a	W	108-67
Dec. 5	Texas-a	W	104-68
Dec. 9	Virginia Tech-b	W	78-62
Dec. 13	Houston	W	84-76
Dec. 20	at Butler	W	103-56
Dec. 22	at Ohio State	W	84-64
Dec. 28	SW Louisiana-c	W	80-59
Dec. 29	Michigan-c	L	79-78
Dec. 30	Hawaii-c	W	101-84
Jan. 4	Cornell	W	98-60
Jan. 7	at N.C. State	W	100-67
Jan. 9	Maryland	W	101-73
Jan. 13	Georgia Tech	W	80-67
Jan. 16	at Clemson	W	82-72
Jan. 20	Virginia	W	80-58
Jan. 24	at Seton Hall	W	70-66
Jan. 27	Florida State	W	82-77
Jan. 30	at Wake Forest	L	88-62
Feb. 3	at Duke	L	81-67
Feb. 6	N.C. State	W	104-58
Feb. 9	at Maryland	W	77-63
Feb. 14	at Georgia Tech	W	77-66
Feb. 17	Clemson	W	80-67
Feb. 21	at Virginia	W	78-58
Feb. 23	Notre Dame	W	85-56
Feb. 27	at Florida State	W	86-76
March 3	Wake Forest	W	83-65
March 7	Duke	W	83-69

ACC TOURNAMENT

DATE	TEAM	WIN/LOSE	FINAL
March 12	Maryland-a	W	102-66
March 13	Virginia-a	W	74-56
March 14	Georgia Tech-a	L	77-75

NCAA EAST REGIONAL

DATE	TEAM	WIN/LOSE	FINAL
March 18	East Carolina-d	W	85-65
March 20	Rhode Island-d	W	112-67
March 26	Arkansas-e	W	80-74
March 28	Cincinnati-e	W	75-68, OT

NCAA FINAL FOUR

DATE	TEAM	WIN/LOSE	FINAL
April 3	Kansas-f	W	78-68
April 5	Michigan-f	W	77-71

a- Charlotte   b- Roanoke, Va.   c- Honolulu   d- Winston-Salem
e- East Rutherford, N.J.   f- New Orleans

when James Forrest scored 27 points to lead Georgia Tech to a 77–75 victory. It took a nailbiting, overtime victory over Cincinnati in the regional final to get to the Final Four, as Reese missed a dunk attempt that would have won it in regulation before the Tar Heels prevailed 75–68 after the extra period. A victory over Kansas and Smith's protégé, Roy Williams, followed in the national semi-finals, setting up North Carolina's meeting with Michigan's vaunted Fab Five of Webber,

Rose, Juwan Howard, Ray Jackson and Jimmy King in the final.

Donald Williams made five of his seven 3-point attempts only to become but a foot-note because of Webber's mistake. The video highlights of the game through the years have showed Webber signaling for his ill-fated timeout, but there's no denying that the opponent that put him and the Wolverines in a such a desperate predicament deserved their national championship.

NATIONAL CHAMPIONS 1981-82

By 1982, North Carolina coach Dean Smith was being subjected to criticism despite the considerable success of his basketball program. After six Final Fours without an NCAA title, the knock on Smith was that his teams couldn't win The Big One. Smith's ability to recruit incredible talent and get players to buy into a team-first system was unquestioned. But some were beginning to question whether that system prevented talented individuals from reaching their full potential and therefore dragged down the entire team. One night in New Orleans, where the Tar Heels won an unforgettable NCAA championship game, quashed that criticism of the man who would become the winningest coach in Division I. Seven-foot freshman Patrick Ewing's domination in the post wasn't enough to keep North Carolina from beating Georgetown 63–62 with one of the greatest collections of talent in the history of college basketball.

The shot that launched a legend: Michael Jordan sinks the game-winner vs. Georgetown.

Freshman Michael Jordan, perhaps the most admired player in basketball history, was a sophomore and made the go-ahead 16-footer with 15 seconds remaining.

James Worthy, a member of the Naismith Hall of Fame, clinched the victory by intercepting Fred Brown's famous, ill-fated pass. Worthy, who scored 28 points in one of the great offensive performances in Final Four history, grabbed the ball on the wing and hustled downcourt to seal Smith's first title.

A third Tar Heel, Sam Perkins, who went on to play 17 seasons in the NBA, scored 25 points with 10 rebounds in a 68–63 victory in the national semifinals over Houston and center Akeem Olajuwon.

The season began with high expectations following a 63–50 loss to Isiah Thomas

NORTH CAROLINA'S 63–62 victory over Georgetown took its place among the classic title games. It was one of 10 NCAA finals decided by one point or in overtime (or both):

YEAR	SCORE
1944	Utah 42, Dartmouth 40, OT
1953	Indiana 69, Kansas 68
1957	North Carolina 54, Kansas 53, 3 OT
1959	California 71, West Virginia 70
1961	Cincinnati 70, Ohio State 65, OT
1963	Loyola (Ill.) 60, Cincinnati 58, OT
1982	North Carolina 63, Georgetown 62
1987	Indiana 74, Syracuse 73
1989	Michigan 80, Seton Hall 79, OT
1997	Arizona 84, Kentucky 79, OT

1981-82 RECORD: 32-2. ACC: 12-2

DATE	TEAM	WIN/LOSE	FINAL
Nov. 28	Kansas-a	W	74-67
Nov. 30	Southern California-b	W	73-62
Dec. 3	Tulsa	W	78-70
Dec. 12	South Florida	W	75-39
Dec. 19	Rutgers-c	W	59-36
Dec. 26	Kentucky-d	W	82-69
Dec. 28	Penn State-e	W	56-50, OT
Dec. 29	Santa Clara-e	W	76-57
Jan. 4	William & Mary	W	64-40
Jan. 6	at Maryland	W	66-50
Jan. 9	Virginia	W	65-60
Jan. 13	at N.C. State	W	61-41
Jan. 16	at Duke	W	73-63
Jan. 21	Wake Forest	L	55-48
Jan. 23	at Georgia Tech	W	66-54
Jan. 27	Clemson	W	77-72
Jan. 30	N.C. State	W	58-44
Feb. 3	at Virginia	L	74-58
Feb. 5	Furman-a	W	96-69
Feb. 6	The Citadel-a	W	67-46
Feb. 11	Maryland	W	59-56
Feb. 14	Georgia-b	W	66-57
Feb. 17	Wake Forest-b	W	69-51
Feb. 20	at Clemson	W	55-49
Feb. 24	Georgia Tech	W	77-54
Feb. 27	Duke	W	84-68

ACC TOURNAMENT

DATE	TEAM	WIN/LOSE	FINAL
March 5	Georgia Tech-b	W	55-39
March 6	N.C. State-b	W	58-46
March 7	Virginia-b	W	47-45

NCAA EAST REGIONAL

DATE	TEAM	WIN/LOSE	FINAL
March 13	James Madison-a	W	52-50
March 19	Alabama-f	W	74-69
March 21	Villanova-f	W	70-60

NCAA FINAL FOUR

DATE	TEAM	WIN/LOSE	FINAL
March 27	Houston-g	W	68-63
March 29	Georgetown-g	W	63-62

a-Charlotte b-Greensboro c-Madison Square Garden
d-East Rutherford, N.J. e-Santa Clara, Calif. f-Raleigh g-New Orleans

and Indiana in the 1981 NCAA championship game. Leading scorer Al Wood was gone, but Perkins and Worthy were strong in the frontcourt and point guard Jimmy Black did a good job distributing the ball. Ranked No. 1 by the Associated Press in the preseason, the Tar Heels won 13 in a row before stumbling at home against Wake Forest. A 74–58 loss to Virginia and Ralph Sampson on Feb. 3 was North Carolina's last defeat, as the Tar Heels finished the regular season 24–2.

North Carolina entered the ACC tournament with its No. 1 ranking restored after having been the nation's top-ranked team for all but five weeks during the season. In the ACC championship game, tournament Most Valuable Player Worthy scored 16 as North Carolina edged Virginia 47–45.

The Tar Heels survived a scare against James Madison in the NCAA Tournament's East Regional, winning 52–50. Victories over Alabama and Villanova vaulted North

Carolina into the Final Four. A fascinating collection of talent was on hand at the Superdome. Georgetown's Ewing and Houston's Olajuwon gave the Final Four a huge presence in the post, and Louisville's collection of veterans were two seasons removed from an NCAA title of their own. It was a stern test of Smith's system, and the Tar Heels passed.

When Black couldn't get the ball to Worthy in the final minute of the championship game, Jordan was wide open for the go-ahead shot. When Smith put on his famous "scramble" defense in hopes of creating a turnover, Brown was pressured into his errant pass. Smith's reward was an NCAA title, and his supporters were thrilled for him.

During the celebration on the court, he told then-assistant Roy Williams that he wasn't any better a coach than he had been a few hours before. But he finally held the hardware that vaulted him into the coaching pantheon.

NATIONAL CHAMPIONS 1956-57

North Carolina's first NCAA title was born on the streets of New York City, which sent a wealth of top talent to Chapel Hill to lift the Tar Heels under coach Frank McGuire.

A native New Yorker who left St. John's to coach North Carolina, McGuire attracted so much New York talent to North Carolina that the path from the Big Apple to Tobacco Road was dubbed "The Underground Railroad." On March 23, 1957, five New York City starters took the court for North Carolina against Kansas and towering center Wilt Chamberlain in the NCAA championship game in Kansas City, Mo.

Lennie Rosenbluth, Pete Brennan, Tommy Kearns, Joe Quigg and Bob Cunningham struggled through a triple-overtime marathon before pulling out a 74–70 victory over Michigan State in the national semifinals. Their stamina would be tested perhaps more than any champion's in NCAA history, as they played three overtimes again in the championship game.

The previous season North Carolina had lost to Wake Forest in the ACC Tournament semifinals but had finished first in the ACC standings and posted an overall record of 18–5. There was excellent talent returning from that team, starting with Rosenbluth, a 6-foot-5 forward who averaged 28 points per game in 1956-57. Chamberlain's size and strength were incomparable, but Rosenbluth earned the nod from the Helms Foundation as National Player of the Year. Rosenbluth helped the Tar Heels gain the No. 1 rank-

1956-57 RECORD: 32-0. ACC: 14-0

DATE	TEAM	WIN/LOSE	FINAL
Dec. 4	Furman	W	94-66
Dec. 8	Clemson-a	W	94-75
Dec. 12	George Washington-b	W	82-55
Dec. 15	at South Carolina	W	90-86, OT
Dec. 17	Maryland	W	70-61
Dec. 20	New York University-c	W	64-59
Dec. 21	Dartmouth-d	W	89-61
Dec. 22	Holy Cross-d	W	83-70
Dec. 27	Utah-e	W	97-76
Dec. 28	Duke-e	W	87-71
Dec. 29	Wake Forest-e	W	63-55
Jan. 8	at William & Mary	W	71-61
Jan. 11	Clemson	W	86-54
Jan. 12	Virginia	W	102-90
Jan. 15	at N.C. State	W	83-57
Jan. 30	at Western Carolina	W	77-59
Feb. 5	at Maryland	W	65-61, 2 OT
Feb. 9	Duke	W	75-73
Feb. 11	at Virginia	W	68-59
Feb. 13	Wake Forest	W	72-69
Feb. 19	N.C. State	W	86-57
Feb. 22	South Carolina	W	75-62
Feb. 26	at Wake Forest	W	69-64
March 1	at Duke	W	86-72
ACC TOURNAMENT			
March 7	Clemson-e	W	81-61
March 8	Wake Forest-e	W	61-59
March 9	South Carolina-e	W	95-75
NCAA EAST REGIONAL			
March 12	Yale-c	W	90-74
March 15	Canisius-f	W	87-75
March 16	Syracuse-f	W	67-58
NCAA FINAL FOUR			
March 22	Michigan State-g	W	74-70, 3 OT
March 23	Kansas-g	W	54-53, 3 OT

a-Charlotte b-Norfolk, Va. c-Madison Square Garden
d-Boston Garden e-Raleigh f-Philadelphia g-Kansas City, Mo.

UNDEFEATED NCAA Division I champions		
YEAR	SCHOOL	RECORD
1956	San Francisco	29-0
1957	North Carolina	32-0
1964	UCLA	30-0
1967	UCLA	30-0
1972	UCLA	30-0
1973	UCLA	30-0
1976	Indiana	32-0

ing in The Associated Press' poll in late January. North Carolina became the first team to finish ACC play undefeated (14–0), with road defeats of South Carolina in overtime and Maryland in double overtime.

In the ACC Tournament semifinals, the nation's top-ranked team trailed Wake Forest by a point in the final minute. Wake Forest fans swore Rosenbluth charged Wendell Carr in the lane on a hook shot with 46 seconds remaining, but Carr was called for a blocking foul.

Rosenbluth made the free throw to complete the three-point play and North Carolina won 61–59 en route to the ACC title.

Rosenbluth wasn't around to save the Tar Heels against Kansas in the NCAA final. He fouled out with a team-high 20 points late in regulation, leaving Quigg to make the winning play in the third overtime. North Carolina trailed by a point when Quigg drove the lane and drew a foul from Chamberlain, who scored 23 points and grabbed 14 rebounds.

With six seconds remaining, Quigg made two free throws to give the Tar Heels a 54–53 victory. Though Chamberlain was the dominating individual in the post, North Carolina outrebounded Kansas 42–28, with Brennan grabbing 11 rebounds to go with 11 points.

The Tar Heels finished 32–0, the second of seven undefeated NCAA champions.

McGuire left for the Philadelphia 76ers after the 1960-61 season and later re-established the New York recruiting pipeline as South Carolina's coach.

★ ★ ★ ★ ★ ★ ★ ★ ★ ★ ★ ★ ★ ★ ★ ★ ★ ★

Three years before leaving North Carolina, McGuire hired Dean Smith as an assistant, matching the Tar Heels with the mentor who would leave his mark on the program for 36 seasons — and beyond.

Coach Frank McGuire and his starting five players get a little workout, March 11, 1957. From left: Bob Cunningham, Lennie Rosenbluth, Tom Kearns, Jon Quigg, Pete Brennan, and McGuire.

Other Great Carolina Teams

1997-98

A gleeful Shammond Williams struck up the Tar Heel band at the Greensboro Coliseum after the buzzer sounded to end an 83–68 victory over Duke in the ACC Championship Game. Tournament Most Valuable Player Antawn Jamison scored 22 points in the final as North Carolina regained the No. 1 ranking in the final Associated Press poll.

Though the Tar Heels finished second to Duke in the ACC regular-season standings, they finished 34–4 and reached the Final Four before losing to Utah in the national semifinals. First-year head coach Bill Guthridge's success illustrated that the North Carolina program would continue to thrive following Dean Smith's retirement after 36 years.

1980-81

Virginia and Ralph Sampson finished in first place in the ACC ahead of Al Wood, James Worthy and the Tar Heels. But North Carolina defeated Maryland 61–60 in the ACC Championship Game and then met Virginia in the national semifinals.

Wood scored 39 points to set a semifinal record that still stands, and Perkins helped hold Sampson to 11 points as North Carolina won 78–65, advancing to meet Indiana in the NCAA title game.

The afternoon of the finals, March 30, John Hinckley Jr. attempted to assassinate President Ronald Reagan. In an anticlimactic final game, Isiah Thomas scored 23 as the Hoosiers won 63–50.

Dean Smith had to wait — but just one more year — for his first NCAA title.

1976-77

Phil Ford and Walter Davis had brilliant seasons as North Carolina placed first in the ACC, won the ACC Tournament and reached the NCAA title game. Ford scored 26 in a 75–69 defeat of Virginia in the ACC final. In the NCAA regional semifinals, Notre Dame led North Carolina by 14 after halftime but couldn't hold on as Ford scored 29 despite a hyperextended elbow in a thrilling 79–77 victory.

In the NCAA championship game, Butch Lee scored 19 as Marquette won 67–59 for the late, great coach Al McGuire, who went on to become one of the nation's most beloved sports broadcasters.

1971-72

South Carolina had dealt the Tar Heels a heartbreaking 52–51 loss in the ACC final the year before, but junior college transfer Robert McAdoo immediately reinvigorated North Carolina.

North Carolina placed first in the ACC during the regular season, and McAdoo was the ACC Tournament's Most Valuable Player as the Tar Heels defeated Maryland 73–64 in the final. McAdoo averaged 19.5 points and Dennis Wuycik, George Karl, Bill Chamberlain and Bobby Jones all averaged 10 or more. Florida State edged North Carolina 79–75 in the national semifinals, and soon afterward McAdoo became the Tar Heels' first underclassman to enter the NBA draft.

1967-68

Only Lew Alcindor and UCLA stopped North Carolina from adding an NCAA title to its first-place ACC finish and ACC Tournament title. Larry Miller had an outstanding season, averaging 22.4 points and capturing ACC Tournament MVP honors. The Tar Heels edged South Carolina 82–79 in overtime in the ACC semifinals, crushed N.C. State 87–50 in the ACC final, then survived a scare against Davidson to win 70–66 in the regional final in Raleigh.

After defeating Ohio State in the national semifinals, North Carolina couldn't stop Alcindor, who scored 34 points and grabbed 16 rebounds to help the Bruins win 78–55.

CAROLINA SUPERLATIVES

Carolina basketball history is littered with moments of greatness — National Championships won, great games played, superior individual efforts, memorable upsets and more. Here is a small sample of that record of achievement.

Great Games

With more than 1,850 victories in its 95-season history, North Carolina has fistfuls of memorable wins. Here are a few great games against opponents from outside Tobacco Road.

NOVEMBER 30, 1982

North Carolina never figured to start its NCAA title defense 0–2, but that was the setting for the home opener in Michael Jordan's sophomore season. After losses away from home to St. John's and Missouri, the Tar Heels trailed visiting Tulane 53–51 when Jordan was called for an offensive foul with four seconds left. An unheard-of 0–3 start seemed all but certain, but Jordan stole the Tulane inbounds pass, and his spinning 24-footer forced overtime. UNC escaped the Green Wave in three extra periods, 70–68.

NOVEMBER 21, 1987

UNC was an underdog to Syracuse in the Hall of Fame Tip-Off Classic, and it was playing without suspended starters J.R. Reid and Steve Bucknall. The Orangemen led by 14 with 15 1/2 minutes to play, but the Tar Heels rallied, forcing overtime on freshman Pete Chilcutt's turnaround jumper at the buzzer. Carolina eventually won 96–93.

MARCH 17, 1990

UNC barely made the NCAA Tournament, earning a No. 8 seed. After dispatching Southwest Missouri State in Austin, Texas, the Tar Heels drew top-seeded and top-ranked Oklahoma. King Rice drew a foul with 10 seconds left and hit one of two free throws to tie the score. The carom on the second shot went out of bounds off Oklahoma, and the Tar Heels drew up a play for the final eight seconds. Rick Fox took a pass from Hubert Davis and drove the right baseline. His off-balance bank shot at the buzzer produced a 79–77 win and sent UNC to its 10th consecutive Sweet 16.

JANUARY 27, 1993

Florida State won its first-ever ACC game a season earlier at the Smith Center, and Pat Kennedy's Seminoles seemed well on their way to another road victory on this night. Florida State led by 21 points early in the second half and still held a 19-point lead with less than nine minutes remaining. But the Tar Heels got hot from outside and buckled down on defense. George Lynch (below) stole Charlie Ward's pass and soared in for a dunk in the final 90 seconds, providing the winning points in an 82–77 win. The Tar Heels closed out the stunned Seminoles with a 28–4 run.

FEBRUARY 18, 1998

The Tar Heels squandered a seven-point, final-minute lead at Georgia Tech, but that only allowed Shammond Williams more opportunities for clutch shooting. Williams finished with 42 points, making two free throws with six seconds left in the first overtime before scoring 12 points alone in the second OT in a 107–100 win in Atlanta.

The team that seemed sunk in the regular season — UNC was 11–8 at one point — also seemed out of good fortune in a Sweet 16 game against Tennessee. The Volunteers led 64–57 with about five minutes left, and UNC center Brendan Haywood had fouled out.

But Ed Cota and freshmen Joseph Forte and Julius Peppers led the comeback in Austin for the eighth-seeded Heels. Forte hit a big outside shot, Cota scored on a pair of drives and Peppers supplied the inside strength in Haywood's absence as UNC finished the 74–69 victory with a 17–5 run.

JANUARY 17, 2004

Everything seemed easy for the Tar Heels in the first half against top-ranked Connecticut, as Carolina took a 50–36 lead. But UConn took the fight to the Tar Heels and led by six in the final minutes. However, Jawad Williams scored 18 points, and Rashad McCants scored UNC's final 10 points, the last ones on a 3-pointer with 6.2 seconds left in an 86–83 triumph at the Smith Center.

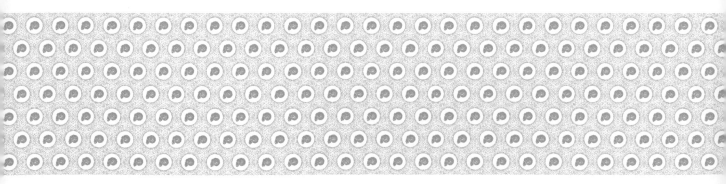

Bob Lewis, shown here vs. Maryland, holds the UNC record for points in a game.

Greatest Moments

QUICK, TRY TO GUESS...

What Tar Heel holds the school record for points in a game. Michael Jordan? Antawn Jamison? Phil Ford? Lennie Rosenbluth?

Good guesses all, but incorrect. The answer: Bob Lewis, an undersized but high-flying forward with a fantastic shooting touch. Lewis, a 6-3, 175-pounder, lit up Florida State for 49 points on Dec. 16, 1965.

Coach Dean Smith said of Lewis: "He was in Billy Cunningham and Vince Carter's class as a leaper."

Of the above candidates for the single-game mark, only Rosenbluth reached 40 as a Tar Heel, doing so five times. And Lewis scored 43 two games prior to setting the school record.

THE KANGAROO KID

Sean May put North Carolina on his shoulders late in the 2005 regular season, carrying the Tar Heels all the way to the NCAA title. Much was made of his scoring and rebounding after a 26-point, 24-rebound performance against Duke in the regular-season finale, an effort that gave him eight consecutive double-doubles.

But as good as May was, he was nowhere close to the UNC record for point and rebound stat-stuffing.

Billy Cunningham, nicknamed the Kangaroo Kid for his leaping, didn't just soar for layups in the 1960s. Cunningham had 40 consecutive double-doubles, the last 20 games of his sophomore season and the first 20 of his junior year. Cunningham averaged 24.8 point and 15.4 rebounds in his career.

THE CATASAUQUA KID

North Carolina had the Kangaroo Kid from 1962-65, and the Catasauqua Kid from 1965-68. That would be Catasauqua, Pa., forward Larry Miller, who once scored 67 points in an ABA game. Miller was solid in his three seasons in Carolina blue, averaging 21.8 points and 9.2 rebounds. He is perhaps best remembered for his play against Duke in the 1967 ACC Tournament final, scoring 32 points on 13-of-14 shooting in an 82–73 victory. "He's some tough rascal," Smith said of Miller, the only player in UNC history to be ACC Player of the Year twice.

CHARLES SCOTT

Just about everyone knew him as Charlie, but Dean Smith was adamant that Scott be called by his full first name. No matter what the name, Scott had a memorable run at UNC, and not just because he was the first black scholarship player at UNC.

Scott was a first-team All-American in 1970. A season before, he scored 29 in the second half of a win over Duke and later hit a last-second jumper against Davidson that sent the Tar Heels to the Final Four.

THE OPENING OF THE DOME

January 18, 1986 is a date that sticks in the minds of Tar Heel fans everywhere. On that day, top-ranked North Carolina opened the spacious Dean Smith Center, defeating No. 3-ranked Duke 95–92 behind 28 points from guard Steve Hale.

The Tar Heels' Smith Center record through the 2005 season (when UNC went 15–0 at the Dean Dome) is 222–43. Money for the construction cost ($34 million) came entirely from private funds, from a total of 2,362 donors.

The 21,750-seat arena replaced Carmichael Auditorium, a 10,000-seat gym in which the Tar Heels were 169–20.

MARCH 15, 1997:
SMITH SETS VICTORY RECORD

It was all set up as soon as the NCAA bracket was announced: The Tar Heels would have to get past Bob Knight and Indiana to give Coach Dean Smith the NCAA Division I record for all-time wins.

Or so everyone thought, with Smith at 875 wins entering the 1997 NCAA Tournament. The top-seeded Tar Heels struggled with Fairfield as Smith tied Adolph Rupp at 876, but Knight's Hoosiers lost to Colorado in Winston-Salem, N.C.

The Buffaloes were no match for UNC, which won 73–56, giving Smith the record. He retired before the next season with 879 victories.

Former Virginia coach Terry Holland said of Smith: "He has been a target for all of us who coached in the ACC to shoot for. ... The Carolina program was the measuring stick to everybody who came into the league."

NBA DRAFT-READY

NBA Draft night has been a roll call of sorts for North Carolina over the years. The Tar Heels have had 89 players drafted and 35 chosen in the first round. That includes a record four underclassmen taken in the first round of the 2005 draft (below).

BEST SHOOTER OF THEM ALL

York Larese was part of the Tar Heels' "underground railroad," the recruiting pipeline Coach Frank McGuire established between Chapel Hill and New York. Larese made 21 of 21 free throws in a game against Duke in 1960, a mark of perfection that remains an ACC record. "I can't ever remember a better shooter in the league," said Vic Bubas, the Duke coach at the time.

Carolina's Fab Four in the 2005 NBA Draft: Rashad McCants, Sean May, Marvin Williams and Raymond Felton.

THE RIVALRIES

Duke-Carolina

It's never over. Never. Even when it should be, even when the two sides in Duke vs. North Carolina should take a vacation from each other and just chill — they can't.

That's the nature of this Tobacco Road tussle, 219 games old but constantly evolving, between a private school born of tobacco money and a public one founded long before James Naismith was born.

Duke's Cameron Indoor Stadium is 10.6 miles from UNC's Dean Smith Center. The players go to the same barbershop, and fan mingling is inevitable, from corporate boardrooms to coffee shops.

Need an example of the never-ending story that is Duke-Carolina?

Take Fourth of July weekend during the summer of 2004, when Blue Devil fans fretted and Tar Heel fans rejoiced as Mike Krzyzewski considered an offer from the Los Angeles Lakers.

Coach K stayed, of course, which gave both sides cause to celebrate. Duke's joy was obvious, as it got to hug tighter on the man who has won three national championships; UNC's, at least from a fan perspective, went like this: When Roy Williams gets his system rolling, it'll be all the more fun to pound Duke with Coach K on the sideline.

A day after K's announcement, word got out that Williams had also talked to the Lakers.

That's the other thing about this rivalry, the constant one-upsmanship.

Both programs are successful, wildly so and not just recently. UNC is No. 2 on the all-time NCAA victory list and has four national titles; Duke is No. 4 and has three NCAA crowns, all since 1991. Duke has 14 Final Four trips, including 10 under Krzyzewski

since 1986; UNC has been to 16 Final Fours, 13 under retired coach Dean Smith.

Krzyzewski says the rivalry is not about the coaches. "We're just driving the bus," he understated.

But he has a point: Duke vs. UNC will continue because of the players in both programs. Michael Jordan played against Johnny Dawkins, Grant Hill against Rasheed Wallace. They gave way to Vince Carter and Antawn Jamison, who played one memorable season against Elton Brand, Shane Battier and Trajan Langdon. When those five clashed, Duke was No. 1 for all three meetings, and UNC was never out of the top four.

The coaches, though, give the rivalry extra oomph. Maryland was becoming Duke's best competition when the Tar Heels plunged to 8–20 in 2001-02. Williams' decision in spring 2003 to leave Kansas and return to his alma mater turned a simmering series into a boiling one.

The rivalry is lava-hot on game nights, especially in sweaty Cameron Indoor, where Duke students unite to become an imposing

and often hilarious sixth man. Those in the front row can almost touch the players.

UNC's fan base traditionally has been less raucous, but the Dean Dome gets down-right deafening when the Blue Devils make the 19-stoplight trip, mostly on U.S. 15-501, from Durham to Chapel Hill.

It is not uncommon for households to be divided — Duke fans watching the game in one room, Carolina fans sequestered else-where. So many people have ties to those on the other side — even the dueling radio voices went to the same high school.

Away from the court, the players are friendly with each other, having become close from the summer recruiting circuit. But that changes the week of the game.

"There's something about that game," said former UNC center Sean May prior to his

senior season. "Like during the game, (he and Duke center Shelden Williams) don't say anything to each other. Normally, we talk a couple times a week. The week coming up to the game, we don't say anything to each other."

The Cameron Crazies camp out months for Carolina tickets, forming a tent village now officially named Krzyzewskiville. North Carolina's fans are no less stoked for each installment, and they show their joy after wins by mobbing Franklin Street. Only NCAA titles match the downtown revelry that follows a win over Duke.

The institutions are cut from different academic cloth, but the programs could pass as twins. They recruit the same players. Anything less than the Final Four is a disappointment. And they are on ESPN more than Nike commercials.

One of those ESPN games was a series benchmark, a 1995 double-overtime nail-

biter at Cameron. UNC survived 102–100, but the game will forever be remembered for Jeff Capel's halfcourt buzzer-beater to force a second overtime.

But that was almost 10 years ago. A more immediate classic was the most recent overtime game, a Duke rally in Chapel Hill capped by Chris Duhon's coast-to-coast drive for a reverse layup.

The series hit a crescendo at the end of the 2004-05 season, when Carolina erased the specter of recent futility against Duke, in the process reclaiming its spot atop college hoops' elite. UNC used an 11–0 run to erase a nine-point deficit with 3:07 left on the way to a 75–73 win over the Devils in Chapel Hill. It was Williams' first win in the series, and quite possibly set a record for decibels inside the Smith Center, especially after Marvin Williams' key putback and free throw gave the Heels the lead for good with 17 seconds

left. The win gave Carolina its 15th outright conference championship and no doubt served as a catalyst for the Heels' title run.

One highlight of that epic evening: May's 26 points and 24 rebounds marked his eighth consecutive double-double, as he became the first UNC player to do so since Mitch Kupchak accomplished the feat during the 1975-76 season. Fitting that it came against Duke.

"It seems like every game tends to outdo itself in the rivalry," Duke assistant coach Chris Collins says. "I'm scared to think what's going to be in store."

UNC-Kentucky

Growing up in Asheville, N.C., North Carolina basketball coach Roy Williams listened to Cawood Ledford's University of Kentucky play by play on late-night radio.

Williams grew up with a healthy respect for the history of college basketball's two winningest programs. Kentucky enters the 2005-06 season with a 1,904–583–1 record. North Carolina stands at 1,860–681.

"It is one of the marquee games that you can ever have in college basketball when Carolina and Kentucky are playing," Williams said.

The teams have met just 27 times, with North Carolina winning 17. There have been some unforgettable games in the series. The day after Christmas in 1981, King Rice scored 22 points as the Tar Heels won 121–110. The 231 points were the most ever in a North Carolina game that didn't go into overtime.

In 1977, the teams met in the NCAA East Regional final at Cole Field House on the University of Maryland campus with a spot in the Final Four at stake. Jack Givens scored 26 points for the Wildcats, but the Tar Heels won 79–72 behind 21 points by Walter Davis, the regional's Most Outstanding Player.

"Coach was the only person that had ever beaten Kentucky... and he said, 'It's about time you get one.'"

NORTH CAROLINA CENTER SEAN MAY

Two of the game's great coaches, Dean Smith and Rick Pitino, matched wits when the teams met again in a regional final in 1995 in Birmingham, Ala. Smith's defense dared Kentucky to shoot 3-pointers, and the Wildcats fell into the trap.

Kentucky attempted 36 threes, making just seven, as Jerry Stackhouse scored 18 with 12 rebounds to lead North Carolina to a 74–61 victory. It was the Tar Heels' sixth straight win in the series, but that streak was soon to end.

After North Carolina and Kentucky began a series in 2000, the Tar Heels lost four in a row by an average of 13.8 points per game. Before the teams met on Dec.

4, 2004, Roy Williams had a pre-game talk with his players about the series.

"Coach was the only person that had ever beaten Kentucky," said North Carolina center Sean May, ". . .and he said 'It's about time you get one.'"

May hit the boards like a man possessed, grabbing 19 rebounds to go with 14 points.

The Tar Heels won 91–78, and Kentucky's players and coaches left Chapel Hill with renewed respect for an opponent they had owned for four years.

"You're not going to find many places tougher than the Dean Dome to play in," said Kentucky coach Tubby Smith.

"You're not going to find many places tougher than the Dean Dome to play in.' KENTUCKY COACH TUBBY SMITH

"It's very intense. ACC basketball, especially the Big Four and *Tobacco road area, it's a topic of conversation almost year round."* BOBBY JONES

UNC-N.C. State

Former North Carolina great Bobby Jones' partner in the Charlotte-based ministry called 2xsalt was disappointed when he saw Carolina blue trim on shirts Jones ordered for the youth the ministry serves.

David Thompson, the N.C. State alumnus who might be the ACC's greatest player ever, told Jones that the next time they ordered shirts, they would be done in red. Jones and Thompson chose to work together and can be civil about the North Carolina-N.C. State rivalry because they became friends during four seasons together with the Denver Nuggets.

But Jones said the rivalry is serious business in North Carolina.

"It's very intense," Jones said. "ACC basketball, especially the Big Four and Tobacco Road area, it's a topic of conversation almost year round."

The teams have met five times in ACC Tournament finals, with North Carolina winning three. The Tar Heels lead the series 132–74, but the Wolfpack has had successful periods in the rivalry.

When the Tar Heels won 68–66 in coach Roy Williams' first game against the Wolfpack in 2004, the players' relief was considerable.

"It is a big win just to beat N.C. State," said point guard Raymond Felton. "It was a four-game winning streak for them."

One of the most memorable games in the series came in the 1987 ACC Tournament final in Landover, Md. North Carolina had gone 14–0 in the conference and would finish 32–4 overall. N.C. State was the ACC Tournament's No. 6 seed, had posted a 6–8 conference record and almost certainly needed to win to reach the NCAA Tournament. Chucky Brown scored 18 and the Wolfpack made all 14 of its free throws, including two by Vinny Del Negro with 14 seconds remaining to win 68–67.

In 1975, the Wolfpack was seeking a third straight ACC Tournament title in Thompson's senior season. But North Carolina point guard Phil Ford scored 24 points and was named Most Valuable Player of the tourna-

ment as a freshman as the Tar Heels won 70–66 and prevented defending national champion N.C. State from advancing to the NCAA Tournament.

It was a humbling end to Thompson's career, as N.C. State declined an NIT invitation. But it didn't stop him from joining forces with a Tar Heel almost 30 years later.

"He's really a very low-key guy and a very humble guy," Jones said. "That makes it fun because you can joke and tease, and we enjoy that."

UNC-Wake Forest

When the Wake Forest player guarding him slipped, Lennie Rosenbluth lowered his shoulder and drove the lane toward perhaps the most controversial three-point play in ACC Tournament history.

Rosenbluth doesn't think he charged Wendell Carr as he scored the winning points in a 61–59 North Carolina victory in the 1957 ACC Tournament.

There would have been no undefeated season and no NCAA championship for the Tar Heels. But the referee called a block, infuriating Wake Forest fans and adding to the ill will in an already heated rivalry.

"Back then it was a big rivalry, because they played us so tough all the time," Rosenbluth said.

Wake Forest ended North Carolina's season in 1956 with a 77–56 drubbing in the ACC Tournament semifinals. At the beginning of practice the next season, Tar Heel coach Frank McGuire reminded the team about that game. Rosenbluth said McGuire never got over that loss.

Although North Carolina leads the series 147–63, Wake Forest has won some big ones.

The most famous might have been the 1995 ACC final, the only time the schools have met to decide the conference championship. Randolph Childress scored 37 points to cap off a record 107-point effort in the tournament, and the Deacons won 82–80 in overtime.

North Carolina has winning streaks of 19, 12, 11 and 11 in the series, but Wake Forest had gone 6–1 in the last seven as the teams entered the 2005-06 season. That included an epic victory at Chapel Hill on Feb. 20, 2003. After being fouled on a 3-point attempt with 1.2 seconds remaining in the second overtime, Chris Paul made two of three free throws to tie the game. Wake Forest won 119–114 in three overtimes; the 233 combined points tied for the second-highest total ever in an ACC game. "I'll remember this one for the rest of my life," North Carolina coach Roy Williams said at the time. "The quality of the play at times was really amazing — shots they made and shots we made."

The next season, the teams met just once — their home and home arrangement quashed by the unbalanced schedule created by ACC expansion — after having played twice each season since 1922. In a strange way, less became more. Wake Forest won 95–82 in a highly charged atmosphere at home.

"It is huge for not only us as a team but for the city of Winston-Salem," said Wake Forest guard Justin Gray. "This game has been circled for us for a long time."

"I'll remember this one for the rest of my life. The quality of the play at times ws really amazing — shots they made and shots we made."
Roy Williams

"I didn't see it go in. I didn't look at the ball at all. I just prayed."

MICHAEL JORDAN ON HIS GAME-WINNER

TALKIN' CAROLINA BASKETBALL

We thought we'd go straight to the source and let some of Carolina's greatest legends share their thoughts about Tar Heel basketball. They put it much better than we could.

"The kid doesn't even realize it yet, but he's part of history now. People will remember that shot 25 years from now." CAROLINA ASSISTANT EDDIE FOGLER AFTER MICHAEL JORDAN'S GAME-WINNING SHOT GAVE THE HEELS A 63-62 WIN OVER GEORGETOWN IN THE 1982 NATIONAL CHAMPIONSHIP GAME

"There is so much I can say about North Carolina and my experiences there. *I forged many special relationships and life-long friendships, received a quality education, and developed both personally and athletically."*
MICHAEL JORDAN

"I was playing the eyeball game. That's what we call it. *You kind of read the eyeball from the back of the defense. When I saw him pick up his dribble, I was like, `Oh, boy, that was a no-no. He's panicking.' That's the worst thing you can do. I saw Jimmy Black had Sleepy (Floyd) denied, so once I saw the pump-fake, I said here's my opportunity, and I jumped out. I just knew he was going to throw it. To whom, I still don't remember."* JAMES WORTHY, ON THE ERRANT PASS THAT SEALED CAROLINA'S 63–62 WIN OVER GEORGETOWN FOR THE NATIONAL CHAMPIONSHIP

"This (championship) is partially theirs. *I feel happy for anyone who's ever worn this jersey."* SEAN MAY, HERO OF NORTH CAROLINA'S LATEST NATIONAL CHAMPIONSHIP, ON THE PLAYERS WHO CAME BEFORE HIM.

"Dean Smith is a better teacher of basketball than anyone else." FORMER UCLA COACH JOHN WOODEN

"He is the greatest coach. If he retired tomorrow, I would vote for him for the Hall of Fame. He told us he would bring us a championship and we did it as a team." RAYMOND FELTON, ON ROY WILLIAMS

"These seniors ... they took me for a heck of a ride." ROY WILLIAMS, AFTER HIS TEAM WON THE NATIONAL CHAMPIONSHIP

"I wouldn't be the person I am today if I hadn't come to Carolina. The whole family atmosphere was special." HUBERT DAVIS

"Night in and night out, every team we played gave us their best, and for myself and my teammates to have that unity, and for me to play three years with the guys I played with, that's something I will cherish for the rest of my life." ANTAWN JAMISON

"I don't think I have ever had a feeling after a big game like *I felt after that last sociology exam. I'm more proud of this than anything I have ever done on the basketball court. This is similar to winning a championship."* JERRY STACKHOUSE, ON EARNING A DEGREE FROM NORTH CAROLINA

131

"He made sure that we knew our teachers by their first names, not just the last names. He'd come and ask you, 'So, what's your teacher's first name?' He'd have a coach who was assigned to be at the front door of very one of our classes, every player." VINCE CARTER, ON DEAN SMITH

"No matter if it was the president of a company or the 15th player on a team or somebody at the airport that picked up our bags, they all felt good about themselves after they met with him, and that's something I would hope that I'd be able to do." LARRY BROWN, ON DEAN SMITH

"I sincerely appreciate having had the opportunity to represent a dynamic institution such as North Carolina and being part of history. Being coached by and playing for Coach Smith and his staff was an awesome experience, one I will always treasure." RASHEED WALLACE

"You do what you have to do to get the win, to make it happen. Whether it's making the steal, getting the rebound, it's all about heart, and our team has heart." RAYMOND FELTON, FOLLOWING CAROLINA'S WIN IN THE NCAA FINALS VS. ILLINOIS

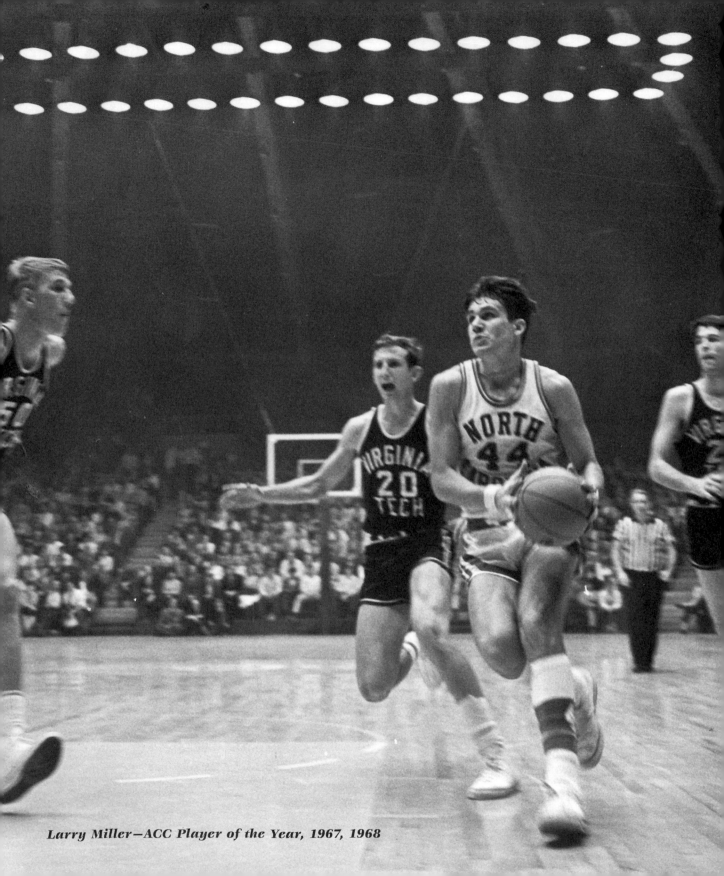

Larry Miller—ACC Player of the Year, 1967, 1968

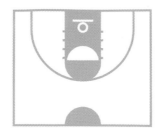

FACTS AND FIGURES

ACC Players of the Year

PLAYER	YEAR
Lennie Rosenbluth	1957
Pete Brennan	1958
Lec Shaffer	1960
Billy Cunningham	1965
Larry Miller	1967, 1968
Mitch Kupchak	1976
Phil Ford	1978
Michael Jordan	1984
Antawn Jamison	1998
Joseph Forte	2001 (co-winner)

National Players of the Year

PLAYER	YEAR	NAMED BY
Jack Cobb	1926	Helms Foundation
George Glamack	1940, 1941	Helms Foundation
Lennie Rosenbluth	1957	Helms Foundation
Phil Ford	1978	U.S. Basketball Writers Association, National Association of Basketball Coaches, *The Sporting News,* John Wooden Award
James Worthy	1982 (co-winner)	Helms Foundation
Michael Jordan	1983	*The Sporting News*
	1984	*The Sporting News,* The Associated Press United Press International, U.S. Basketball Writers Association, National Association of Basketball Coaches, *Basketball Weekly,* John Wooden Award, Naismith Award
Kenny Smith	1987	*Basketball Times*
Jerry Stackhouse	1995	*Sports Illustrated*
Antawn Jamison	1998	The Associated Press, John Wooden Award, Naismith Award, *The Sporting News,* National Association of Basketball Coaches, U.S. Basketball Writers Association, CBS/Chevrolet, Basketball America, *Basketball Times, Basketball News*

Regional Championships

NCAA-Record 15 Final Fours

YEAR	REGION	REGIONAL SITE	CHAMPIONSHIP GAME RESULT
1946	East	New York, N.Y.	North Carolina 60, Ohio State 57
1957	East	Philadelphia, Pa.	North Carolina 67, Syracuse 58
1967	East	College Park, Md.	North Carolina 96, Boston College 80
1968	East	Raleigh, N.C.	North Carolina 70, Davidson 66
1969	East	College Park, Md.	North Carolina 87, Davidson 85
1972	East	Morgantown, W.Va.	North Carolina 73, Penn 59
1977	East	College Park, Md.	North Carolina 79, Kentucky 72
1981	West	Salt Lake City, Utah	North Carolina 82, Kansas State 68
1982	East	Raleigh, N.C.	North Carolina 70, Villanova 60
1991	East	East Rutherford, N.J.	North Carolina 75, Temple 72
1993	East	East Rutherford, N.J.	North Carolina 75, Cincinnati 68 (OT)
1995	Southeast	Birmingham, Ala.	North Carolina 74, Kentucky 61
1997	East	Syracuse, N.Y.	North Carolina 97, Louisville 74
1998	East	Greensboro, N.C.	North Carolina 75, Connecticut 64
2000	South	Austin, Texas	North Carolina 59, Tulsa 55
2005	Syracuse	Syracuse, N.Y.	North Carolina 88, Wisconsin 82

Rebounding Leaders

Sam Perkins	1980-84	1,167
George Lynch	1989-93	1,097
Billy Cunningham	1962-65	1,062
Antawn Jamison	1995-98	1,027
Mitch Kupchak	1972-76	1,006
Brad Daugherty	1982-86	1,003
Eric Montross	1990-94	941
Rusty Clark	1966-69	929
Ademola Okulaja	1995-99	890
Scott Williams	1986-90	861

Assists

Ed Cota	1996-2000	1,030
Kenny Smith	1983-87	768
Phil Ford	1974-78	753
Raymond Felton	2002-05	698
Derrick Phelps	1990-94	637
King Rice	1987-91	629
Jeff Lebo	1985-89	580
Jimmy Black	1978-82	525
Steve Hale	1982-86	503
Matt Doherty	1980-84	446

Scoring

Phil Ford	1974-78	2,290
Sam Perkins	1980-84	2,145
Lennie Rosenbluth	1954-57	2,045
Al Wood	1977-81	2,015
Charles Scott	1967-70	2,007
Larry Miller	1965-68	1,982
Antawn Jamison	1995-98	1,974
Brad Daugherty	1982-86	1,912
Walter Davis	1973-77	1,863
Bob Lewis	1964-67	1,836

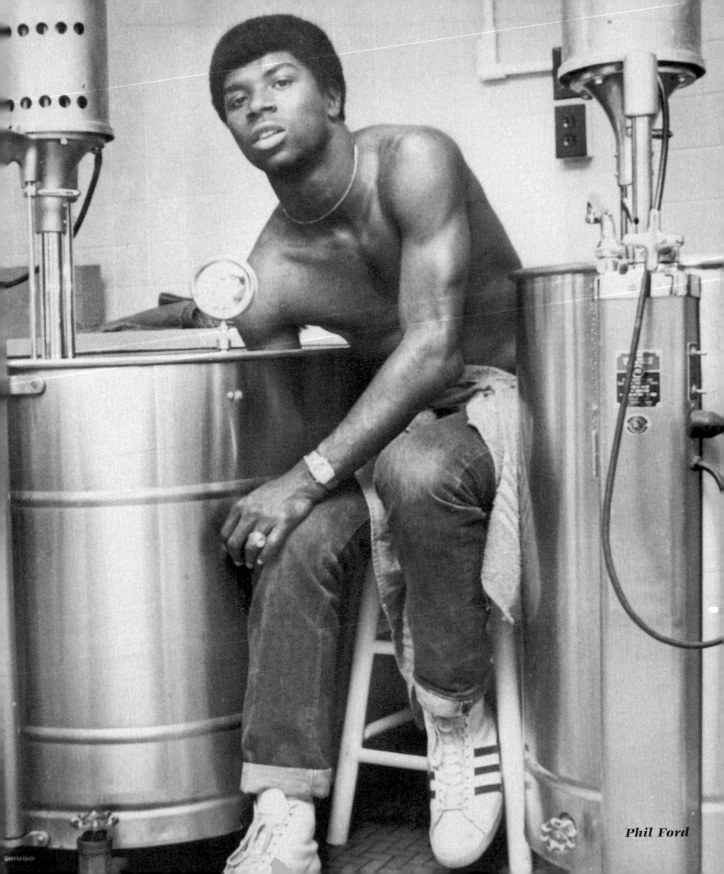

Phil Ford

First Round Draft Picks

YEAR	PLAYER	TEAM	SELECTION
1957	Lennie Rosenbluth	Philadelphia Warriors	6
1958	Pete Brennan	New York Knicks	4
1960	Lee Shaffer	Syracuse Nationals	5
1965	Billy Cunningham	Philadelphia 76ers	4
1972	Bob McAdoo	Buffalo Braves	2
1974	Bobby Jones	Houston Rockets	5
1976	Mitch Kupchak	Washington Bullets	13
1977	Walter Davis	Phoenix Suns	5
1977	Tommy LaGarde	Denver Nuggets	9
1978	Phil Ford	Kansas City Kings	2
1979	Dudley Bradley	Indiana Pacers	13
1980	Mike O'Koren	New Jersey Nets	6
1981	Al Wood	Atlanta Hawks	4
1982	James Worthy	Los Angeles Lakers	1
1984	Michael Jordan	Chicago Bulls	3
1984	Sam Perkins	Dallas Mavericks	4
1986	Brad Daugherty	Cleveland Cavaliers	1
1987	Kenny Smith	Sacramento Kings	6
1987	Joe Wolf	Los Angeles Clippers	13
1989	J.R. Reid	Charlotte Hornets	5
1991	Rick Fox	Boston Celtics	24
1991	Pete Chilcutt	Sacramento Kings	27

YEAR	PLAYER	TEAM	SELECTION
1992	Hubert Davis	New York Knicks	20
1993	George Lynch	Los Angeles Lakers	12
1994	Eric Montross	Boston Celtics	9
1995	Jerry Stackhouse	Philadelphia 76ers	3
1995	Rasheed Wallace	Washington Bullets	4
1998	Antawn Jamison	Toronto Raptors	4
1998	Vince Carter	Golden State Warriors	5
2001	Brendan Haywood	Cleveland Cavaliers	20
2001	Joseph Forte	Boston Celtics	21
2005	Marvin Williams	Atlanta Hawks	2
2005	Raymond Felton	Charlotte Bobcats	5
2005	Sean May	Charlotte Bobcats	13
2005	Rashad McCants	Minnesota Timberwolves	14